The Fraternal Complex in the Middle East

The Fraternal Complex in the Middle East extends group and family psychoanalytic concepts to formulate hypotheses on the psychic functioning of nation-states as very large families.

Focusing on the history of Lebanon as a nation-state, the emergence and role of Hezbollah in Lebanon, the Israeli-Palestinian conflict and the rise and role of Hamas in the Palestinian sociopolitical field, Hana Salaam Abdel-Malek interprets historical events and conflicts as symptoms of unconscious group and family psychic functioning. This perspective offers insight into the unconscious forces that drive conflicts, especially for mediators and peace architects working on Middle East issues. Salaam Abdel-Malek also proposes a group psychoanalytic approach to provide peacemakers and peacebuilders with complementary mediation tools that can foster transformation and shield or decontaminate them and their practices from the potentially traumatic elements of their profession.

The Fraternal Complex in the Middle East will be of interest to group analysts, psychoanalysts in practice and in training, psychologists and mediators. It will also be relevant for readers interested in peacemaking, social conflict and conflict transformation.

Hana Salaam Abdel-Malek is a clinical psychologist and psychoanalyst, and a member of the Paris Psychoanalytical Society and the International Psychoanalytical Association. She works in private practice in Beirut, specialising in couples, families and groups. She has practised law and received training in negotiation, mediation and peacemaking.

The Fraternal Complex in the Middle East

Group and Family Psychoanalysis for Peacemaking and Peacebuilding

Hana Salaam Abdel-Malek

Routledge
Taylor & Francis Group
LONDON AND NEW YORK

Designed cover image: Cover image illustrated by Fadi Salaam

First published 2025
by Routledge
4 Park Square, Milton Park, Abingdon, Oxon, OX14 4RN

and by Routledge
605 Third Avenue, New York, NY 10158

Routledge is an imprint of the Taylor & Francis Group, an informa business

© 2025 Hana Salaam Abdel-Malek

British Library Cataloguing-in-Publication Data
A catalogue record for this book is available from the British Library

ISBN: 9781032900254 (hbk)
ISBN: 9781032900247 (pbk)
ISBN: 9781003545842 (ebk)

DOI: 10.4324/9781003545842

Typeset in Times New Roman
by codeMantra

Contents

Permissions

This book is a revised version of the author's six articles:

- 'Birth of a nation-state: A battle for boundaries or dialogue?' published in 2020 in *International Journal of Applied Psychoanalytic Studies*
- 'A group psychoanalytic approach to international mediation', published in 2021 in *International Journal of Applied Psychoanalytic Studies*
- 'A group psychoanalytic approach to the analysis of peacemakers' practice', published in 2022 in *International Journal of Applied Psychoanalytic Studies*
- 'Hezbollah: Lebanon's identified patient?' published in 2022 in *International Forum of Psychoanalysis*
- 'Israeli–Palestinian conflict: The *archaic fraternal complex*', published in 2023 in *International Journal of Applied Psychoanalytic Studies*
- 'A group psychoanalytic approach to the *Social Dreaming Matrix: A found and created* device', published in 2023 in *British Journal of Psychotherapy.*

These articles are reproduced here with the kind permission of Wiley publishing and Taylor & Francis publishing.

The Writesonic and DeepL platforms were used for language enhancement. The Quillbot platform was used to check for plagiarism in Chapter 5. No artificial intelligence (AI) platform was used for content generation.

About the author

Hana Salaam Abdel-Malek is half Lebanese and half Greek, and was born in Germany. She spent her early years in different countries before settling in Lebanon, where she has lived most of her life. She is a clinical psychologist and psychoanalyst, and a member of the Paris Psychoanalytical Society, the International Psychoanalytical Association (IPA) and the International Association for Couple and Family Psychoanalysis. She works in private practice in Beirut, specialising in couples, families and groups.

She studied psychology at the American University of Beirut in Lebanon, where she taught for several years. She then studied law at the Lebanese University and practised for a few years in the early 1990s before returning to clinical psychology and psychoanalysis. She holds a Doctorate in Humanities (Psychology), a Diploma in Advanced Specialised Studies (Diplôme d'Études Supérieure Spécialisée) in Clinical Psychology and Psychopathology, a University Diploma in Psychoanalytic and Systemic Family Therapy and a University Diploma in Psychoanalytic Psychodrama from Saint-Joseph University in Beirut, Lebanon, where she also taught for several years. She continued her training at the Cercle d'Études Françaises pour la Formation et la Recherche: Approche Psychanalytique du Groupe, du Psychodrame, de l'Institution (CEFFRAP), founded in 1962 by Anzieu, Bejarano, Kaës, Missenard and Pontalis, which was dissolved in 2014. She also received training in hosting social dreaming matrices from the *Social Dreaming International Network Organisation*.

Her personal and professional history, coupled with the fact that she lives in Lebanon, a country that has been ravaged by war in one form or another for the past 40 years, has spurred her interest in using her clinical and psychoanalytic expertise beyond the confines of private clinical practice to contribute to peacemaking and peacebuilding. To familiarise herself with the field of mediation, she completed the Certificate in Mediator Skills Training offered by the Centre for Effective Dispute Resolution (CEDR), the Certificate in International Conflict Mediation and Peacemaking offered by Oxford Process and CEDR, the Practitioner's Certificate for Consultancy and Change offered by the Tavistock Institute for

Human Relations, and the Certificate in Negotiation and Leadership and the Negotiation and Leadership-Change Management course offered by Harvard Law School Executive Education.

With the expertise she has gained, she aims to extend the perspectives and tools of couple, family and group psychoanalysis to the field of mediation to complement the current strategies of peacemakers by working on the unconscious dynamics at play in dialogues. She was runner-up for the 2009 IPA Tyson Prize and co-winner of the *British Journal of Psychotherapy 2021 Rozsika Parker Prize* (Post Qualification Path). She has published several articles in international psychoanalytic journals and her prose poem 'Fireworks' was published in the IPA book *Mind in the Line of Fire*.

Preface

I was ten. I huddled with my brother in my aunt's silver Vauxhall. Bullets flew overhead—birds chirping in mid spring. Automatic rifles and .50-calibre machine guns. We screamed. We covered our ears. 'Stay down,' my aunt said. She drove, her chin touching the wheel. Perhaps she could dodge a flying bullet. Perhaps. Perhaps. Palestinian guerrillas and the Lebanese army fought in the streets of Beirut.

I turned 12. I looked at the pictures on the front page of our Lebanese newspaper, Al-Nahar. It was covered with pictures of men with their eyes banded in black. Who were these young men? These photogenic models of beauty stood before my eyes as I stared, mesmerised. I thought they were ancient statues chipped by time: men with the tips of their noses cut off; men with their ears cut off; men with their tongues cut off. And then there were the naked men with their penises cut off. Cut. Cut. Action. Castration enacted. Lebanese brothers mutilated each other. Fully conscious. Or so they thought: Cut. Cut. Cut each other. Cut for the love of Lebanon. Which Lebanon? Cut in the name of God. Oh, my God. Oh, my God.

13 April 1975. The Lebanese Civil War had begun. The Syrians were called upon to stop the war. They complied. But the sectarian conflict continued. For 15 years it did. In different forms it did. I spent those years hiding in corridors and stairwells. Lebanese militia guerrillas lurked on street corners, firing rocket-propelled grenades at each other. Palestinian refugees massacred Lebanese Christians and Lebanese Christians massacred Palestinians. Syrians kidnapped Lebanese Christians. Syrians kidnapped any Lebanese who opposed them. They occupied Lebanon. After all, Lebanon had been part of Greater Syria during the Ottoman Empire. The Syrians ruled. Lebanon was deemed unfit to govern itself.

I was 19. It was 9 am and I was tucking the white sheets into the foot of my bed when I felt sucked into a vacuum. A rocket had hit the house opposite my father's veranda; the Israeli attack on West Beirut had begun. 'Operation Peace for the Galilee', 14 June 1982. What looked like a sandstorm set us in motion. We rushed to the basement, my father, my brother and I, taking the stairs by twos and threes. It was three floors down and I felt like I was entering the womb of the earth. We would be safe there. Who is not safe in a womb? But this was no womb. It was a big empty space, grey and dark like a tomb. A rocket hit the car park above us. It did not explode. I threw myself on the ground, kicking in all directions. 'I don't want to die', I cried. We came out of the grave. Risen. Israelis stood at the corner of the street in surveillance. We stole glances at them, expecting to find extraterrestrials.

I got married. I had a daughter. She was nine months old. Our Army General launched the War of Liberation against the Syrian army in West Beirut. I fled. I returned. Our Army General launched the War of Elimination against the Christian Lebanese Forces. It was not nearby. What a relief. In times of war, it is a relief to be a few streets away. I had learned to distinguish between the sound of bombs flying over our heads and the sound of bombs falling on our heads.

Hostilities ceased. Time passed. I became a psychoanalyst. A patient lay on my couch, and I listened to her with benevolent neutrality. An explosion reverberated; the glass panes rocked. It was Valentine's Day, 2005. Former Prime Minister Hariri had been assassinated. The Lebanese blamed Hezbollah. The Lebanese blamed the Syrians. The Cedar Revolution uprising broke out. 'Syrian forces out. Out'. The Syrians withdrew from Lebanon after almost three decades. So long. Farewell. Adieu. Adieu. To you and you and you.

Israel invaded Lebanon. In again. This time, it was the 2006 War against Hezbollah. Links were attacked. Bridges. Cut. Cut. Cut. Lebanon and its capital rumbled for 34 days. The Israeli troops withdrew. 'Divine victory', Hezbollah said. Divine. Divine. The consequences were divine.

I turned 57. I was sitting in a café with my neighbour, looking out at the open sea. The earth trembled beneath us, and my cappuccino twirled like a dervish. Shuddering. An explosion echoed. A thunderstorm rumbling in midsummer. 'It's nothing. Fireworks stored in the port of Beirut', I was told. Fireworks? Fireworks mutated into one of the most powerful man-made non-nuclear explosions in history. Illegally stored ammonium nitrate had exploded. So had Hezbollah rockets. 'Israeli drones bombed the area', some said. Were they drones? Who knows?

What I do know is that corruption has infested Lebanon, gnawing away at its parliamentary, executive and judicial systems like a weevil. The 'jewel', the 'Paris of the Middle East', has been transformed into a failed nation-state. Electricity shines on us people for one hour a day. Water quenches our thirst once a week. Gaz is a rare commodity for which we have to queue from the wee hours of the morning to fill our car tanks, oblivious to the risk of knife fights and gunshots. And the Lebanese Pound, the Pound is in free fall. The terminal drop, indeed. People are drowning in the Mediterranean, fleeing Lebanon in search of a better life.

I was 60. Hamas launched an attack on southern Israel. Hezbollah supported Hamas. They are brothers after all. Hezbollah sent rockets into northern

Israel. Israel returned the favour. Fireworks. Fireworks. South Lebanon is playing with fire.

I am 61. All of Lebanon is in flames. In the name of brotherhood. The whole region could burn. In the name of brotherhood. World War III?. Nonsense. Nonsense. My mind is frozen. I must find sense. The child, the adolescent, the adult, the psychoanalyst in me has to make sense. My mind has been forged in the line of fire. I have to circumvent the aegis of Thanatos, with its decathexis and its attacks on linking effects. I put my thoughts into articles. I linked them through the dynamics of complicated separation-individuation and the *archaic fraternal complex*. I have collected these articles in this book. My way of working through trauma, of mentalising the enactments of my country. My way of sharing my understanding. Perhaps there is a way to make peace. Perhaps. Perhaps.

Introduction

Prior to the First World War, present-day Lebanon, Syria, Jordan, Palestine and Israel were all governed by the Ottoman Empire, Bilad el-Cham (the countries of Damascus) or Greater Syria. After the end of the First World War and the collapse of the Ottoman Empire, the Sykes-Picot Agreement of 1916 divided the Arab provinces of the Empire into British and French zones of influence. At the San Remo Conference in 1920, the League of Nations, recognising that not all parts of the Middle East were ready for full independence, mandated Ottoman Greater Syria to France, which eventually partitioned it to create the two present-day states of Syria and Lebanon.

Iraq and Palestine were mandated to Britain, and Transjordan was added in 1921. The purpose of these mandates was to provide administrative advice and assistance until these newly created nation-states could stand on their own (Becker Lorca, 2016; Evans, 2018). However, since then, these nation-states have been plagued by violence and tragedy and have struggled to define their borders, become autonomous and live in harmony and peace. Furthermore, these nation-states have been burdened by defensive ideological positions that exclude the other and otherness, leading to further escalation of conflict and violence.

The Israeli-Palestinian conflict is one of the most persistent and intractable in the world and has been generalised as an Arab-Jewish and Muslim-Jewish conflict. Israelis and Palestinians are perpetually 'in the traumatic' (Silverman & Parger, 2004), each identifying as a victim and compulsively repeating the cycle of violence in which death has become a way of life (Grossman, as cited in Silverman & Parger, 2004). Lebanon has also been in a state of turmoil since its inception in 1920; its viability as a nation-state is threatened by its current economic crisis and the systematic erosion of its legislative, executive and judicial functions. Syria and Iraq have also been in a state of violent upheaval for more than a decade.

The intractable conflicts of the Middle East have been extensively analysed from political, ethnic, religious, psychological and psychoanalytical perspectives. However, despite these broad and in-depth analyses, which have been undertaken to help understand and transform the various conflicts in

DOI: 10.4324/9781003545842-1

the Middle East, the various parties remain mired in repetitive and vicious cycles of destructive wars and conflicts. In this book, I propose to extend individual, family and group psychoanalytic theories and concepts such as separation-individuation (Mahler, 1958) and the *archaic fraternal complex* (Kaës, 2008) to explain the unconscious dynamics that may underlie some of the conflicts in the Middle East. After all, social and political relationships are built on people's internalised family models and relationships. Social and political conflicts are in part projections of these internalised representations.

In this book, I reflect, in particular, on Lebanon's history as a nation-state, the rise and role of Hezbollah in Lebanon and the Israeli-Palestinian conflict. In my analysis, I build on Vamik Volkan's (1999, 2004, 2009a, 2009b, 2013) insights into the psychology of large-group identity and psychological borders, narcissism, regression and destructive processes, the impact of the transgenerational transmission of trauma, the reactivation of chosen traumas and glories, as well as time collapse (when the present reactivates prior traumas, leading to collusion between the past and the present) on national and international relations. I propose to extend his work by using group and family psychoanalytic theories to formulate hypotheses about the psychic functioning of a nation-state as a very large family. Thus, I interpret historical events as symptoms of this unconscious group and family psychic functioning.

In my analysis, I do not record historical events, establish their veracity or use them to support a political position. Nevertheless, given my background as a Lebanese child, I acknowledge that I do not have sufficient distance, and I am aware of the difficulty of psychoanalysing my Lebanese family. I also acknowledge, as Picco has noted (Rifkind & Picco, 2014), that readers on different sides of the conflict may perceive me as 'being closer to the other side since the only "impartiality" a side at war usually recognises is partiality on their side' (p. 13). Furthermore, in walking the slippery slope of applied psychoanalysis (Abella, 2016), I do not discredit the geopolitical, socio-economic or cultural interpretations of the conflict. Nevertheless, as Anzieu (2021) has argued, psychoanalysis must be applied whenever the unconscious surfaces. Proposing a psychoanalytic interpretation is not antinomic to geopolitical, socio-economic or cultural interpretations. Material and psychoanalytic interpretations address different layers of a problem in a logic of complementarity rather than in an 'either/or' sense. I hope that my psychoanalytic reflections will provide new insights into the Israeli-Palestinian compulsive enactments.

Through these psychoanalytic reflections, I hope to contribute to both peacemaking and peacebuilding. Warring siblings in such conflicts may gain insight that allows them to mourn their original symbiotic state and narcissistic link to a primal mother, to separate and individuate and to break free from the rigid fanatical ideologies to which they are oriented. Of course, this psychic work, whether at the peace table or at the grassroots level, is a long process that may take decades, if not generations, before violent conflict is transformed and sustainable peace is fostered.

I have divided this book into two parts. Part I focuses on the psychoanalytic analysis of conflict in the Middle East. Part II focuses on a group psychoanalytic tool for peacemaking and peacebuilding.

In Part I, I begin by clarifying the group and family psychoanalytic theoretical framework on which I base my analysis. In Chapter 2, I discuss Lebanon's history and the ways in which Lebanon's group psychic reality underlies its civil war and its struggle to build a viable independent nation-state. In Chapter 3, I interpret the rise of Hezbollah and its role in Lebanese sociopolitical life from a group and family psychoanalytic perspective. In Chapter 4, I extend group and family psychoanalytic theories to analyse the unconscious dynamics that may underlie the Israeli-Palestinian conflictual relationship, interpreted in the light of the biblical narrative of Abraham, his wives (Sarah and Hagar) and his sons (Isaac and Ishmael). In Chapter 5, I examine the rise of Hamas and its involvement in the longstanding Israeli-Palestinian conflict through the lens of group and family psychoanalysis. In Chapter 6, I reflect on the national and international dialogues surrounding these issues.

In Part II, I begin with an explanation of the psychoanalytic group apparatus and group psychodrama. In Chapter 8, I consider whether a group psychoanalytic approach could complement the current strategies of peacemakers by working through the unconscious dynamics at play in dialogues to promote the transformation of conflictual relationships. In Chapter 9, I suggest that a group psychoanalytic approach to the analysis of peacemakers' practice can offer mediators the space to explore, elaborate and symbolise the unconscious dynamics underlying their practices to shield or decontaminate themselves and their practices from the potentially traumatic elements inherent in the bellicose situations they deal with at the peace table. In Chapter 10, I propose a group psychoanalytic Social Dreaming Matrix as another complementary tool for peacemakers and peacebuilders.

I hope that the reader will discover an innovative conceptualisation of Middle Eastern conflicts and peacemaking and peacebuilding strategies. The proposed interpretation can provide a basis for further analysis, particularly in understanding the dynamics of other mandated Middle Eastern states that emerged after the dissolution of the Ottoman Empire, such as Syria and Iraq.

References

Abella, A. (2016). Psychoanalysis and the arts: The slippery ground of applied analysis. *Psychoanalytic Quarterly, 85*(1): 89–119. https://doi.org/10.1002/psaq.12059

Anzieu, D. (2021). Psychoanalysis still. *International Journal of Psychoanalysis, 102*: 109–116.

Becker Lorca, A. (2016). *Mestizo international law: A global intellectual history 1842–1933.* Cambridge: Cambridge University Press, New Edition.

Evans, M. (2018). *International law.* Oxford: Oxford University Press.

Kaës, R. (2008). *Le Complexe Fraternel [The fraternal complex].* Paris: Dunod.

Mahler, M. S. (1958). Autism and symbiosis, two extreme disturbances of identity. *International Journal of Psycho-Analysis, 39*: 77–82.

Rifkind, G., & Picco, G. (2014). *The fog of peace: The human face of conflict resolution.* London: I.B. Tauris & Co. https://doi.org/10.5040/9780755602957

Silverman, H., & Parger, J. (2004). The Middle East crisis: Psychoanalytic reflections. *International Journal of Psycho-Analysis, 85*(5): 1265–1268. https://doi.org/10.1516/0020757042259511

Volkan, V. D. (1999). Psychoanalysis and diplomacy: Part III. Potentials for and obstacles against collaboration. *Journal of Applied Psychoanalytic Studies, 1*: 305–318. https://doi.org/10.1023/a:1023019619160

Volkan, V. D. (2004). *Blind trust: Large groups and their leaders in times of crisis and terror.* Charlottesville, VA: Pitchstone Publishing.

Volkan, V. D. (2009a). Large-group identity, international relations and psychoanalysis. *International Forum of Psychoanalysis, 18*(4): 206–213. https://doi.org/10.1080/08037060902727795

Volkan, V. D. (2009b). The next chapter: consequences of societal trauma. In: P. Gobodo-Madikizela & C. Van Der Merwe (Eds.), *Memory, narrative and forgiveness: Perspectives of the unfinished journeys of the past* (pp. 1–26). Cambridge: Cambridge Scholars Publishing.

Volkan, V. D. (2013). Large-group-psychology in its own right: Large-group identity and peace-making. *International Journal of Applied Psychoanalytic Studies, 10*(3): 210–246. https://doi.org/10.1002/aps.1368

Part I

Group and family psychoanalytic analysis of the Middle East conflicts

Chapter 1

Group and family psychoanalytic theoretical frameworks

To constitute a group identity that structures the psychic life of its members and their intersubjective links, the citizens of a country must seal unconscious alliances with each other, which is the case for members of all groups, who engage in these processes on an unconscious level. Dangerous material or thoughts are repressed, rejected, denied or erased (Kaës, 2010), and members renounce the direct realisation of destructive drives and instead identify with the symbolic father rather than the primal father of the primitive horde as Freud (1913, 1921, 1930, 1939) argued. Their fraternal pact becomes founded on the law and the fundamental prohibitions of incest, cannibalism and murder (Kaës, 2014). Because of these *structuring alliances* (Kaës, 2014), group members fulfil unconscious desires that would be impossible for them to fulfil individually. The group becomes a whole, endowed with a psychic apparatus that is irreducible to the individual apparatuses of its constituent members or the psychic space of their intersubjective links.

The group apparatus maintains specific unconscious processes and effects that are different from those of its members. It influences and is influenced by the psychic reality of its members and by their intersubjective links (Kaës, 2000). In a group, members speak of their individual unconscious dynamics, those of the group as a whole and those of the intersubjective links within the group. As a *work group* (Bion, 1961), the group apparatus contains, forms and transforms its own emotional experiences and psychic reality as well as those of its members and their intersubjective links. It is also reciprocally influenced by the psychic realities of its members and by their intersubjective links (Kaës, 2007). However, when faced with traumatic experiences or unspoken anxieties, affects or phantasies, a work group transforms into one that functions with a defensive basic assumption mentality (Bion, 1961)—the tacit underlying assumptions on which the group is based, its latent aspects or unconscious wishes, fears, defences, phantasies, impulses and projections. This is also true of families, which are the prototypes of groups (Freud, 1921).

A nation is 'a body of people recognised as an entity by virtue of their historical linguistic or ethnic links' (The New Lexicon Webster's Dictionary of the English Language, 1992), inhabiting a defined territory as a relatively

DOI: 10.4324/9781003545842-3

autonomous living unit with a specific coherent identity and internal dynamics. Accordingly, it is an ensemble or whole, that is, a total object, with its own *group psychic envelope* and group psychic apparatus (Kaës, 2000) or group mentality (Bion, 1961). The latter is irreducible to the individual apparatuses of its constituent citizens or to the psychic space of their intersubjective links. A nation has its own psychic functioning and unconscious processes that are distinct from those of its members and that occur only at the group level. Furthermore, a nation has its own form of group narcissism (Hery, 2002; Lemaire, 2001, 2002), which allows it to function as a narcissistic entity and that provides it with a sense of group identity expressed through the first-person plural, we. As Freud (1921, p. 116) stated, a group is 'a number of individuals who have put one and the same object in the place of their ego ideal and have consequently identified themselves with one another in their ego'. To understand the psychic functioning and unconscious processes of a nation, I take into account, similar to Kaës (2010), the psychic reality of the the individual members of a nation, that of their intersubjective links and that of the group itself.

Geographical borders or *skin-ego*

Anzieu (1979, p. 23) hypothesised that 'the ego is constituted as a containing envelope, a protective barrier and a filter of exchanges, as a result of proprioceptive and epidermal sensations and the internalisation of skin identifications'. The *skin-ego* is thus a narcissistic envelope that distinguishes the Me from the not-Me. Anzieu (1993) extended the concept of *skin container* or *psychic envelope* to groups and families, arguing that these groups have a common skin that contains *psychic envelopes* that define their identity. These *psychic envelopes* organise the unconscious psychic functioning of the group and family and structure the links between their members.

As a large family group, for a nation to fulfil its primary tasks, it must clearly delineate its geographical boundaries to form a group and family psychic envelope and a cohesive identity that serves a maternal-containing function and acts as a shield for its members, providing them with a sense of security and belonging (Anzieu, 1993). In this chapter, I reflect on the psychological link between a nation's ability to demarcate its borders and constitute its body envelope and its ability to develop a solid identity as an independent nation-state. 'The ego is first and foremost a bodily ego; it is not merely a surface entity but is itself the projection of a surface' (Freud, 1923, p. 26). I propose that when a nation becomes a sovereign political nation-state, it has, similar to an infant, metaphorically separated and individuated (Mahler, 1958) and developed a solid ego. Thus, when a nation-state fails to clearly delineate its geographical borders or body envelope, its family *skin-ego* will remain perforated, preventing it from properly distinguishing between the Me and the not-Me or the inside and the outside. Accordingly, its body will feel fragmented, its history will reflect a dysfunctional group and its family dynamics will manifest as a battle over boundaries and a struggle to define a viable nation-state or solid ego.

Dysfunctional family dynamics and *incestuality*

A dysfunctional family, like an infant on the autism spectrum or experiencing psychosis who has not achieved the separation-individuation stage of developmental (Mahler, 1958), is characterised by boundary confusion between the Me and the not-Me. As such, it remains in a state of *primary narcissism* (Freud, 1914), which refers to a historically objectless stage of undifferentiation that precedes object recognition. Hery (2002) has proposed the concept of *group primary narcissism*. When *primary narcissism* is at play, differences cannot be tolerated because they imply an object-subject separation. As a result, the family has difficulty working through *primal mourning* (Racamier, 1992), which is a universal original psychic process, not to be confused with bereavement or depression. Through *primal mourning*, the ego mourns its symbiosis with the mother and renounces total possession of the object, which leads to the differentiation and arrangement of object relations and forms the basis of a strong, secure and autonomous ego. Family dynamics are thus governed by *incestuality*—a term developed by Racamier (1995) to designate a pregenital functioning that is distinct from incestuous enactments. *Incestuality* combats the desire to separate and individuate and maintains a confusion of boundaries between the Me and the not-Me; it is related to the narcissistic link to the primal mother. *Incestuality* has features of incest without necessarily incestuous enactment. It eschews intrapsychic conflicts and the work of mourning. It denies phantasies of desire and death, and intolerable affect. *Incestuality* is dominated by the death drive and repetition compulsion. Primary process thinking and enactment characterise the functioning of groups and their members.

The integrity and security of the self and the identity of each member are threatened, and because it is unable to contain its internal tensions, the family feels threatened by them. Its psychic apparatus becomes characterised by a pregenital, narcissistic and *incestual* mode of functioning (Racamier, 1995), with incestuous features but without necessarily actual incestuous enactment. Hence, the narcissistic link to the primal mother opposes the desire to separate and individuate.

To combat family-group intrapsychic conflicts, *incestuality* serves the death instinct and the compulsion for repetition and omnipotence. Furthermore, *incestuality* prevents the definition of family relationships and denies phantasies of desire and death, as well as feelings of disillusionment, helplessness and mourning. *Incestuality* paralyses the mental processes of the family by attacking and subverting the interplay of primary and secondary thought processes. The mental functioning of individual members then becomes dominated by the pleasure principle, discharge, deficient symbolisation, massive projective identifications and enactments. Family functioning is, accordingly, predominated by a defensive basic assumption mentality (Bion, 1961), and sibling relationships become governed by the dynamics of the archaic form of the *fraternal complex*.

Sibling relationships and the *fraternal complex*

To understand the economy and dynamics that organise sibling and group relationships, Kaës (2008) proposed the concept of the *fraternal complex*. It is an unconscious intrapsychic triangular organisation (ego-mother/father-sibling) that regulates relationships on a horizontal level and is distinct from the Oedipal complex, which regulates relationships on a vertical axis (ego-mother-father). In line with Kaës, Mitchell (2006, 2013a, 2013b, 2014) examined sibling and lateral relationships on a horizontal axis that operates independently but interacts with the parent-child vertical axis. This horizontal axis has unique unconscious dynamics that are not simply extensions of the vertical axis.

According to Kaës (2008), the *fraternal complex* manifests in either the symbolic and Oedipal or the archaic form. The symbolic and Oedipal version is characterised by the interplay of hatred, envy and jealousy on the one hand, and love, ambivalence and identification with the other sibling on the other. In the archaic version of the complex, this interplay is split, with hatred, envy and jealousy prevailing. The infant retains the imago of the fecund primal mother and entertains the archaic phantasy of regaining the original symbiotic state by returning to the smooth and unobstructed maternal womb emptied of its contents (Chasseguet-Smirgel, 1987, 1990). The infant therefore entertains phantasies of envious attacks on the mother's womb and the imaginary babies it contains. The sibling is perceived either as a narcissistic double or as a part object rather than as a whole person. They are reduced to the status of appendage to one's own imaginary body or the shared imaginary body of the mother (Kaës, 2008), rather than a whole person. According to this logic, the part object must be eliminated. Sibling rivalry takes a deadly turn. The biblical and Koranic primal fratricidal phantasy of Cain against Abel (Qabil against Habil) is reactivated.

In contrast to Kaës, who emphasised the imago of the archaic mother and the envy of her womb full of babies, Mitchell (2006, 2013a, 2013b, 2014) emphasised the traumatic impact that the arrival of the newborn sibling has on the older infant. Initially, the toddler expects the new baby to be an extension of themselves, a continuation of their own babyhood. However, despite similarities, the new baby is distinctly different and symbolises the 'other'.

As a result, the toddler feels replaced and their identity as the one and only 'Majesty the Baby' is usurped. They temporarily feel like a 'no one', resulting in a narcissistic injury. With the arrival of the newborn, the infant simultaneously experiences a desire for narcissistic sexual union with the similar and a desire to eliminate the different. The sibling trauma triggers a 'kill or be killed' dynamic. According to Mitchell, these incest and murder desires are different from the intergenerational dynamics of the Oedipus complex and have different consequences.

The mother forbids sibling incest and murder (2006, 2013a, 2013b, 2014). The infant must love the new baby but must not treat them as an extension of themselves; any form of sexual behaviour with the baby is strictly forbidden, as is any form of violence against the baby, who has now taken a significant place in the family. This 'law of the mother' creates an internal conflict between desires and prohibitions, with the threat of punishment if these prohibitions are violated. This law does not completely repress or eliminate these tabooed desires (the Oedipus complex), but instead integrates them into social norms. It transforms the pre-social infant into a social child, transitioning from family-centred interactions to those within peer groups. This process involves splitting violent impulses and distinguishing between friends and enemies.

When siblings fail to do the work of *primal mourning*, the *fraternal complex* is transformed into the archaic form (Kaës, 2008). Consequently, their desire to unite with the object ignites their claustrophobic anxieties, while their desire to separate from it triggers their agoraphobic fears. To protect themselves from these anxieties, the siblings, in a defensive magical idealisation and megalomania, deny their kinship and entertain the self-engendering phantasy instead (Caillot, 2003; Racamier, 1989, 1992, 1995). They have the phantasy that they are born of themselves, that they have no parents and that they are their own progenitors, or even the progenitors of their parents. This denial of dependency allows them to cling to a sense of infantile omnipotence, seeing themselves as the creators of their existence and the world, usurping the roles traditionally played by parents and ancestors. In this scenario, Oedipus is displaced, and the difference between sexes and generations is erased. The self-engendering phantasy expresses pathological narcissism and *incestual* dynamics that serve the death drive (Racamier, 1989). In this phantasy, the siblings experience the omnipotence of being God-like to cope with the feelings of impotence caused by the trauma.

Sibling relationships become characterised by recurrent conflicts and perverse manoeuvres (Caillot, 2003), that is, by the intention to manipulate and dominate the other, deny their qualities and disqualify their perceptions and feelings. Hatred and violence towards the sibling are not only the result of an Oedipal displacement towards the parents, but as they are primarily derived from having been held in the same bodily and maternal psychic space, they are the result of an unconscious primitive desire to expel the rival sibling, who is perceived as an intruder, as well as the result of the desire to be the sole possessor of the mother's womb and her phallus (Kaës, 2008). In this archaic form of the *fraternal complex*, the conflict becomes a radical life-and-death struggle, with the need to preserve oneself and confirm one's phallic narcissism at the expense of obliterating the other, who is perceived as a part object (Kaës, 2008).

It becomes difficult to acknowledge individual differences and individuality because individuation and separation threaten the very existence of the family members, triggering fears of death and murder. 'Be like me, see what I see, think what I think, and feel what I feel' becomes 'take my side'. Thus, the family's emotional system triangulates into perverse coalitions against the other, and its power structure becomes chaotic, abusive, inadequate or paradoxical, a structure that is characterised by alienation in a single reading of the world. Communication is often a dialogue of the deaf, also known as the expression of the *incestual*, that are indifferent to rules because they are perceived as forms of aggression. The archaic talionic law replaces the social paternal law. It is an *incestual* law that prohibits without protecting (Racamier, 1995).

The ideological position

In dysfunctional group and family dynamics, the structuring ideology, which is a set of beliefs that organise group life, providing a rationale for its existence and origin and a sense of collective identity, common purpose and belonging (Kernberg, 2003), transforms into a *closing ideology* (Kaës, 2016).

A *closing ideology* is a systematic construction that purports to provide a universal and total explanation according to a unique principle of causality that is beyond all doubt and possible criticism. The omnipotence of the idea as an absolute belief dominates. The cruel group ideal ego replaces the group's ego ideal. Feelings of shame, humiliation, resentment and injured identities are transmitted across generations. This is a paranoid vision of the world that excludes the other and otherness, with conspiracy theories providing an ideological response to misery and shame (Kaës, 2016). It is an unconscious attempt towards a narcissistic reorganisation and a prosthesis for the group's narcissistic fragility, replenishing the narcissistic haemorrhage of perforated containers (Benghozi, 2016).

A *closing ideology* is an alienating and defensive unconscious alliance (Kaës, 2014). It reflects *incestual* dynamics because it denies reality and avoids the psychic work of *primal mourning*. It collapses singular psychic apparatuses into a massified body with an undifferentiated group apparatus. Individuals are subjugated to the idea, the ideal and the idol, as a triple insurance against collapse, loss and breakdown (Kaës, 2016). Individuals build their identity by relying on the identity of the group. Internal objects cannot organise psychic life, archaic violence is unbridled and relationships become governed by fear (Freud, 1921). The group creates the idol—an idealised, faultless and all-powerful part object—to deny feelings of lack, anxiety and destructivity (Kaës, 2016). In this way, the group maintains the omnipotence phantasy, which Anzieu (1984) called group illusion. As a form of group paranoia, a *closing ideology*, like the paranoia of a family member, denotes loyalty conflicts (Boszormenyi-Nagy & Spark, 2013).

The identified patient

Additionally, to protect the family group from the risks of ego disintegration and fragmentation and the terror that accompanies the process of individuation, as well as to escape the catastrophic anxieties they generate, the family often unconsciously chooses a scapegoat, which reflects its basic assumption mentality (Bion, 1961). A member sacrifices themselves by becoming an identified patient—the spokesperson for the non-elaborated family suffering that threatens the survival of the group, such as problematic separation-individuation and loyalty. They carry the family's projected split-off destructive drives and focus on both the negative aspects of family functioning and its hope for a better future. They play the paradoxical role of the *scapegoat/Messiah* (Houzel & Catoire, 1994). They simultaneously maintain the family's fragile cohesion and enable its psychological survival by diverting its conflicts onto themselves while at the same time worrying, persecuting and embarrassing their family, signalling its failure.

Final remarks

In this chapter, I have conceived of a nation-state as a large family with its own *skin-ego*, narcissism, psychic apparatus and functioning. To understand its unconscious dynamics, especially the dysfunctional ones, I have highlighted certain central family psychoanalytic concepts, which I will elaborate on in the following chapters in the hope of contributing to the understanding of intractable and violent national and international conflicts.

References

Anzieu, D. (1979). The sound image of the self. *International Review of Psychoanalysis, 6*: 23–36.

Anzieu, D. (1984). *The Group and the Unconscious.* London: Routledge & Kegan Paul.

Anzieu, D. (1993). Le moi-peau familial et groupal [The family and group skin-ego]. *Gruppo, Revue de Psychanalyse Groupale, 9*: 9–18.

Benghozi, P. (2016). Clinique identitaire de la radicalisation idéologique et Djihad dans les organisations incestueuses et incestuelles [An identity-based clinical approach to ideological radicalisation in incestuous and incestual organisations]. *Revue de Psychothérapie Psychanalytique de Groupe, 67*(2): 51–66.

Bion, W. R. (1961). *Experiences in groups and other papers*. London: Tavistock. https://doi.org/10.4324/9780203359075

Boszormenyi-Nagy, I., & Spark, G. M. (2013). *Invisible loyalties*. London & New York: Routledge.

Caillot, J.-P. (2003). Envie, sacrifice et man'uvres perverses narcissiques [Envy, sacrifice, and perverse narcissistic manoeuvres]. *Revue Française de Psychanalyse, 67*: 819–838. https://doi.org/10.3917/rfp.673.0819

Chasseguet-Smirgel, J. (1987). L'acting out:' Quelques réflexions sur la carence d'élaboration psychique ['Acting out:' Some reflections on the lack of psychic elaboration]. *Revue Française de Psychanalyse, 51*: 1083–1099.

Chasseguet-Smirgel, J. (1990). Reflections of a psychoanalyst upon the Nazi biocracy and genocide. *International Review of Psycho-Analysis, 17*: 167–176.

Freud, S. (1913). Totem and taboo. In: J. Strachey (Ed.), *The standard edition of the complete psychological works of Sigmund Freud, Volume XIII (1913–1914)* (pp. 7–162). London: The Hogarth Press.

Freud, S. (1914). On narcissism. In: J. Strachey (Ed.), *The standard edition of the complete psychological works of Sigmund Freud, Volume XIV (1914–1916): On the history of the psycho-analytic movement, papers on metapsychology and other works* (pp. 67–102). London: The Hogarth Press.

Freud, S. (1921). Group psychology and the analysis of the ego. In: J. Strachey (Ed.), *The standard edition of the complete psychological works of Sigmund Freud, Volume XVIII (1920–1922): Beyond the pleasure principle* (pp. 65–144). London: The Hogarth Press.

Freud, S. (1923). The ego and the Id. In J. Strachey (Ed.), *The standard edition of the complete psychological works of Sigmund Freud, Volume XIX* (pp. 1–66). London: Hogarth Press.

Freud, S. (1930). Civilization and its discontents. In: J. Strachey (Ed.), *The standard edition of the complete psychological works of Sigmund Freud, Volume XXI (1927–1931): The future of an illusion, civilization and its discontents and other works* (pp. 57–146). London: Hogarth Press.

Freud, S. (1939). Moses and monotheism: Three essays. In: J. Strachey (Ed.), *The standard edition of the complete psychological works of Sigmund Freud, Volume XXIII* (pp. 1–138). London: The Hogarth Press.

Hery, P. (2002). Une blessure narcissique groupale [A group narcissistic injury]. *Revue de Psychothérapie Psychanalytique de Groupe, 38*(1): 19–35. https://doi.org/10.3917/rppg.038.0019

Houzel, D., & Catoire, G. (1994). *La Famille comme Institution [The family as an institution]*. Paris: Apsygée.

Kaës, R. (2000). *L'appareil Psychique Groupal [The group psychic apparatus]*. Paris: Dunod.

Kaës, R. (2007). *Linking, alliances, and shared space*. London: The International Psychoanalytic Association.

Kaës, R. (2008). *Le Complexe Fraternel [The fraternal complex]*. Paris: Dunod.

Kaës, R. (2010). *La Parole et le Lien: Associativité et le Travail Psychique dans les Groups [The speech and the link: Associativity and psychic work in groups]*. Paris: Dunod.

Kaës, R. (2014). *Les Alliances Inconscientes [Unconscious alliances]*. Paris: Dunod. https://doi.org/10.3917/dunod.kaes.2014.01

Kaës, R. (2016). *L'idéologie, l'idéal, l'idée, l'idole [The ideology, the ideal, the idea, the idol]*. Paris: Dunod. https://doi.org/10.3917/dunod.kaese.2016.01

Kernberg, O. F. (2003). Sanctioned social violence: A psychoanalytic view-Part I. *International Journal of Psycho-Analysis, 84*(3): 683–698. https://doi.org/10.1516/002075703766644913

Lemaire, J.-G. (2001). Un certain retour du nous dans la culture et la psychanalyse [A certain return of we in culture and psychoanalysis]. *Dialogue, 154*(4): 3–10. https://doi.org/10.3917/dia.154.0003

Lemaire, J.-G. (2002). Introduction au concept de narcissisme groupal [Introduction to the concept of group narcissism]. *Revue de Psychothérapie Psychanalytique de Groupe, 38*(1): 7–18. https://doi.org/10.3917/rppg.038.0007

Mahler, M. S. (1958). Autism and symbiosis, two extreme disturbances of identity. *International Journal of Psycho-Analysis, 39*: 77–82.

Mitchell, J. (2006). From infant to child: The sibling trauma, the rite de passage, and the construction of the "Other" in the social group. *Fort Da, 12*: 35–49.

Mitchell, J. (2013a). Siblings: Thinking theory. *Psychoanalytic Study of the Child, 67*: 14–34.

Mitchell, J. (2013b). The law of the mother: Sibling trauma and the brotherhood of war. *Canadian Journal of Psychoanalysis, 21*.145–159.

Mitchell, J. (2014). Siblings and the psychosocial. *Organizational and Social Dynamics, 14*: 1–12.

Racamier, P. C. (1989). *Antœdipe et ses destins [Antoedipus and its destinies]*. Paris: Apsygée.

Racamier, P. C. (1992). *Le Génie des Origines [The genius of origins]*. Paris: Payot and Rivage.

Racamier, P. C. (1995). *L'inceste et l'incestuel [The Incest and the incestual]*. Paris: Éditions du Collège.

The New Lexicon Webster's Dictionary of the English Language (Deluxe Encyclopedic ed.). (1992). New York, NY: Lexicon Publications, Inc.

Chapter 2

Birth of a nation-state
A battle for boundaries or dialogue?

On Sunday 13 April 1975, Lebanese Christian Phalangists ambushed and opened fire on a bus carrying Palestine Liberation Organisation (PLO) members and sympathisers returning from a political rally, killing most of the passengers, including unarmed women and children. This bloody incident inflamed long-standing sectarian hatreds and mistrust and sparked a civil war in Lebanon that lasted until 1990. The Lebanese Civil War was in fact a series of conflicts, including the two-year war from April 1975 to November 1976; the interval of failed peace efforts; Israeli invasions and Syrian interventions, as well as internal conflicts between November 1976 and June 1982; the Israeli invasion and its aftermath from June 1982 to February 1984; the internal wars of the late 1980s; and finally, the inter-Christian wars of 1988 to 1990.

Birth, physical boundaries and the psychic envelope

Before the First World War, Lebanon was part of Ottoman Greater Syria; it referred to the semi-autonomous Mutasarrifate of Mount Lebanon and was inhabited by the Maronite and Druze religious minorities, who fought each other repeatedly. In 1920, the San Remo Conference gave League of Nations Mandate for the Ottoman Greater Syria to France, which partitioned it to create modern-day Syria and Lebanon. To create a viable Greater Lebanon state, the French moved the Lebanese-Syrian border to the Anti-Lebanon Mountains, which historically and culturally belonged to Syria. They then merged the Maronite Christian semi-autonomous Mutasarrifate of Mount Lebanon with the predominately Muslim coastal cities of Beirut, Tripoli, Sidon and Tyre, which had originally been administered as part of the province of Syria (Salibi, 1988). Thus, a Mutasarrifate territorial entity inhabited by Christian Maronite and Druze religious minorities under the protection of the Ottoman Empire became Lebanon, a nation-state territorial entity with a constitutional law of reason. However, religious kinship and transmission continued to take precedence over the institutions of the nation-state and

DOI: 10.4324/9781003545842-4

the law of reason. Metaphorically speaking, the father-religion remained in conflict with the motherland.

The borders of Greater Lebanon were the Mediterranean Sea to the west, the new Syria to the north and east and British-mandated Palestine to the south. The borders of the three countries met at the village of Ghajar, a tripoint in the Golan Heights region. Moreover, under the 1947 United Nations (UN) Partition Plan, British-mandated Palestine was to be divided into the Jewish state of Israel and the Arab state of Palestine; the latter would share the Lebanese southern frontier.

This plan was contested by the Arabs, and after Israel was declared in 1948, an Arab-Israeli war broke out. Eventually, an armistice border agreement, the Green Line, was reached and the intended borders of the Jewish-Arab states were modified (Sella, 1986). The borders of the three countries, Greater Lebanon, Syria and British-mandated Palestine, born from the womb of the Ottoman Empire and impregnated by the father of the Occident, remain unclear in some regions to this day. These three countries were metaphorically triplets, born deformed, and when Israel declared its independence in 1948, another baby was born out of British-mandated Palestine with intertwined borders.

It is as if Lebanon as a nation-state was born prematurely by caesarean section with the intervention of France, and since then it has been struggling to survive as a nation-state, its viability always at risk, because despite the desire of the Maronite Christian Lebanese subgroup to create a nation-state under the protection of France, there was no national consensus on the matter, and the final creation of Greater Lebanon was mainly determined by French interests, which did not correspond to the vision of any Lebanese political party (Traboulsi, 2012). Lebanon enacted its need to demarcate its borders.

During the 1975 civil war, Lebanon's capital Beirut was divided. The Green Line, also known as the Demarcation Line, separated the predominantly Muslim West Beirut from the predominantly Christian East Beirut, and eventually the Sunnite area from the Shiite area. This line ran from the north of Beirut to the south, along with Damascus Street (Calame & Charlesworth, 2011). By referring to this border as the Green Line, the Lebanese may have unconsciously enacted in their capital the need for Lebanon to define the disputed part of its 1949 Green Line border with Israel. By creating this border on Damascus Street, which refers to the Syrian capital, they may also have enacted through their capital the need for Lebanon to demarcate its disputed borders with Syria, albeit at the expense of internal splitting.

After the creation of Israel in 1948 and the ensuing Palestinian-Israeli war, Arab Palestinian guerrillas who had fled or been expelled from their homes infiltrated Lebanon from the Syrian border and began attacking Israel from the south. The confusion of borders between Lebanon and Palestine/Israel apparently allowed these fighters to maintain the illusion that their attacks were launched from within their Palestinian territories. The areas of

British-mandated Palestine bordering Lebanon were supposed to be part of the future Arab Palestine, according to the 1947 UN Partition Plan.

Palestinian guerrilla cross-border raids led Israel to invade southern Lebanon in March 1978 and occupy a large part of its southern territory until May 2000, when it was forced to withdraw due to unrelenting military resistance, mainly from the Shiite brothers (Hezbolla). In this invasion, Operation Litani, Israel established a new border, the Red Line, geographically delimited in the north by the Litani River, to create a new security zone on its northern border. It implicitly expressed its desire to modify the Sykes-Picot Treaty of 1916 and the San Remo Agreement of 1920 (Eshel, 2001). These cross-border raids also led the Christian militia, the Free Lebanon Army, led by the Christian officer Major Haddad, to seek Israeli assistance. Israel provided military and economic aid by opening its border under its Good Fence Policy. In 1979, Haddad proclaimed the Free Lebanon State, which did not receive international recognition (Jabbra & Jabbra, 1983). Lebanon thus lived in a state of confused borders and internal splitting and fragmentation, with various cantonal states emerging within the state.

Following the Israeli invasion in 1978, Lebanon sought the support of the UN, which in Resolution 425 demanded that Israel cease its military action against Lebanon and withdraw its forces from its territories. However, Israel did not withdraw its troops until 2000. To verify that this withdrawal complied with the resolution, and in the absence of an international consensus on Lebanon's borders, the UN had to draw a temporary blue withdrawal line between the two countries, more or less in line with the Anglo-French agreement of 1923. This line considered certain mountainous areas on the border to be occupied Syrian territory, while Lebanon claimed them to be Lebanese. Consequently, Lebanon did not recognise the Israeli withdrawal from its territories and refused to deploy its troops or allow the UN to deploy troops on the southern border. To liberate these supposedly Lebanese territories, Hezbollah, the Lebanese Shiite resistance force, began to attack Israel across this Blue Line border. Israel counter-attacked.

Meanwhile, Syria, which entered Lebanon in 1976 to end the Lebanese civil war, maintained a military presence until 2005. This led the UN Security Council, in its Resolution 1559 of 2004, to call on Lebanon to establish its sovereignty over all its territory. The resolution also called on foreign forces (Syria) to withdraw from Lebanon and stop interfering in Lebanon's internal affairs and ordered all Lebanese and non-Lebanese militias to disband. Syria did not withdraw its forces from Lebanon until April 2005, under pressure from the Lebanese anti-Syrian Cedar Revolution, sparked by the assassination of former Lebanese Prime Minister Rafik Hariri (Jaafar & Stephan, 2009; Safa, 2006). However, Syria continued to interfere in Lebanon's internal affairs even after establishing diplomatic relations with Lebanon in October 2008 for the first time since both countries gained independence from France in the 1940s and officially recognising Lebanon's individuality as a separate entity.

Between 2011 and 2017, the Syrian civil war spilled over into Lebanese territory, where opponents and supporters of the Syrian regime fought each other. Many Lebanese Sunnite Muslims supported the Syrian rebels, while many Lebanese Shiite Muslims, including Hezbollah, supported and fought alongside the Syrian regime, fuelling Lebanon's sectarian divisions, perverse alliances and Israeli-Lebanese cross-border conflict.

Recently, Lebanon's maritime borders with Israel were demarcated because of potential gas resources, but they remain disputed between Syria and Lebanon.

Incestual group psychic functioning and the archaic fraternal complex

Lebanon's border wars point to its state of group *primary narcissism* (Freud, 1914), which denotes an objectless stage of undifferentiation that precedes the recognition of the object. These wars also point to its symbiotic unity with Syria, its mother nation, and to its difficulties in symbolically processing *primal mourning*, through which the ego mourns its symbiosis with the mother and renounces total possession of the object, leading to the differentiation and arrangement of object relations and forming the basis of a strong, secure and autonomous ego (Racamier 1992). Lebanon, however, refuses to recognise the UN's temporary blue demarcation line. Lebanon cannot delineate a well-defined body envelope that would support the development of a group and family *psychic envelope* necessary for the differentiation of the Me and not-Me or the inside and outside. As a result, Lebanon has remained in an *incestual* state of fusion and confusion with its neighbours. To cross international borders is unconsciously to cross the incest barrier into the mother (Falk, 1974). Lebanon's sense of self has remained fragmented, its psychic envelope incapable of acting as an excitation shield to contain and transform the primitive transgenerational impulses and anxieties of its national group and individual citizens into symbolic thought. Typical of *incestual* family functioning, enactment became paramount and a state of war reigned.

During the civil war, the two divided areas of the Lebanese capital slowly became homogeneous as the Christian minorities of West Beirut migrated to East Beirut and the Muslim minorities of East Beirut moved to West Beirut. In East Beirut, the slogans of a Christian republic, federalism and partition prevailed (Krayem, 1997), while in West Beirut, with its Muslim majority, the militias and political parties called for a secular leftist or Arabist regime. The Syrian Social Nationalist Party, founded by the Christian son Antoun Saadeh, also sought a Greater Syria. Accordingly, the desire to maintain the illusion of omnipotence and idealised undifferentiation as a defence against primitive anxiety serves as another manifestation of *incestuality* (Racamier, 1995), which refers to a pre-genital function, distinct from incestuous enactments, that combats the desire to separate and individuate and maintains a confusion of boundaries between the Me and the not-Me; it is related to the narcissistic link to the primal mother.

The need for the Lebanese to maintain the illusion of undifferentiation lies in Lebanon's history, which has been marked by centuries of sectarian persecution and violence. Persecution and annihilation anxieties have been passed down through the generations.

Before the First World War, Lebanon referred to Mount Lebanon, a mountainous area used in the early centuries as a refuge by the persecuted Maronite and Druze religious minorities. With the decline of the Ottoman Empire, the European powers, to gain a foothold in the region and to contain the centuries-old animosity and fighting between the Maronites and the Druze, divided Mount Lebanon into a northern district under a Christian Kaymakam and a southern district under a Druze Kaymakam. However, the conflict between the two religious communities continued, culminating in the massacres of the civil war of 1860. To prevent a recurrence of such conflicts, an international commission reunited Mount Lebanon in 1861, separating it from Syria and making it a semi-autonomous Mutasarrifate under Christian rule (Lutsky, 1969). Between 1982 and 1984, Maronites and Druze fought in the Chouf area in what became known as the Mountain War. Although the 1984 war had contemporary geopolitical roots, including the hegemony of right-wing Christian militias over the local Druze population and the Christian militias supported by the Israeli Defence Forces, which occupied the area from 1982 to 1984, this war evoked the ghosts of the past, with the Maronites and Druze unconsciously re-enacting their centuries-old history and compulsively repeating the massacres of 1860.

Lebanon's psychic apparatus mobilised the basic fight-or-flight assumption described by Bion (1961) and expressed a paranoid-schizoid position (Klein, 1958). The Lebanese siblings were unable to in a good enough manner to create a unified ego and nation-state total object. Unable to abandon *primary narcissism*, they remained as part objects, split into sectarian and confessional subgroups. These groupings may have given them an infantile narcissistic power and provided them with a cohesive group identity that compensated for the absence of a clear Lebanese identity (Volkan, 2004). Loyalty to the sectarian group, its idolised leader and its ideology gave them a sense of containment and certainty. This conscious sociopolitical and religious ideology expresses collective defensive and pathogenic unconscious alliances to freeze traumatic elements associated with a catastrophe; it helps the siblings to avoid a difficult simultaneous identification with the victim and the executioner (Kaës, 2014). This atmosphere of idealisation and megalomania is typical of *incestuality*.

In creating idealised and idolised leaders who could provide security for the Lebanese, perhaps replacing their ego ideal (Freud, 1921) and the psychic envelope of their deficient nation-state, the siblings enacted the basic assumption dependency as described by Bion (1961). These leaders seem to be remnants of the early primal fathers before the Ottoman Empire and later during the period of the provinces of the Ottoman Empire before they formed Greater Lebanon. These leaders acted similarly to the omnipotent fathers of the primitive horde, narcissistically investing in a phallic defence against the horror of castration and the recognition of kinship, albeit at the expense of establishing a symbolic order (Kaës, 2016). The Lebanese seem to have sought to recover their *primary narcissism* in a new form of ego ideal (Freud, 1914).

The Lebanese sibling subject-other splitting demonstrates how primitive infantile dynamics influence groups and sociopolitical life. When individuals construct their identity by relying on the collective identity of the sectarian group, internal objects fail to structure psychic life and archaic violence is unleashed. In addition, mutual bonds cease to exist and fear is triggered (Freud, 1921). Thus, perverse and sadomasochistic narcissistic manoeuvres characterised Lebanese relations, and Lebanese sectarian groups promoted themselves defensively at the expense of manipulating, devaluing and denying the narcissistic autonomy of the other groups. As a result, citizens mutilated each other. Tongues, ears and penises were cut off. As part objects, they re-enacted the unconscious fratricidal phantasies of the *archaic fraternal complex* (Kaës, 2008), in which each sibling unconsciously entertains the phantasy of returning to the mother's womb and aspires to be her phallus and the exclusive owner of her space. Battles of elimination, fratricidal massacres and assassinations were at the forefront of the civil war, beginning with the Bus Massacre and continuing with the massacres of Karantina and Damour, the Palestinian refugee camps of Tel al-Zaatar, Sabra and Shatila and the massacres of the Mountain War, among others. These massacres show how unconscious alliances are formed when alienating ideals and cruel idols triumph. Through these pathogenic alliances underlying sociopolitical and religious ideologies, the Lebanese denied their identification with the executioner as well as the traumatic features of their actions (Kaës, 2014). Their identification with the victim position may have relieved them, through projection, of denied devalued parts of the self, envied internal objects, and intolerable narcissistic affects, including shame, anger, helplessness, despair, terror and depressive and paranoid fears.

The lack of clear borders between the triplet countries may have triggered the archaic phantasy of conjoined twins or, in this case, conjoined triplets of the *fraternal complex* (Kancyper, as cited in Legorreta, 2013). Lebanon's narcissistic attachment to Syria as the primal mother contrasts with its desire to separate and individuate. Since the creation of Greater Lebanon, a Lebanese subgroup has aspired to return to symbiotic bliss with Syria, the conjoined sister or mother country, and to reunite with it. Although this aspiration may be driven by prephallic phantasies of confraternity and complementarity (Kancyper, 2011), this subgroup may have sought to form a magical, omnipotent and inseparable brotherhood united by *primary narcissism*. Another subgroup (mainly Maronite Christians) identified themselves as ethnically distinct from Lebanon's Arab neighbours and sought a Christian state under the protection of France, their tender, loving mother. In calling for a Christian state under the protection of France, the Maronites may have been expressing an archaic anxiety of annihilation passed down through generations, as they had forged strong links with the French crusaders when they were persecuted. The Lebanese sectarian siblings, in an expression of the *archaic fraternal complex*, entertained the phantasy of returning to the mother's womb, thus avoiding the work of *primal mourning*. The Lebanese parties oscillated between narcissistic and anti-narcissistic investments in each other, enacting the basic assumption pairing as described by Bion (1961). They have repeatedly formed pathological alliances with each other and with external forces against each other to protect themselves from separation, claustrophobic, agoraphobic and annihilation anxieties.

The Lebanese children may have gone to war as a defensive reaction to their desire for narcissistic fusion. During the Lebanese civil war, early hatreds and rivalries over the nurturing breast and the struggle to occupy the motherland alone were revived. As each sibling may have aspired to be unique in the eyes of their mother, this could only be achieved by eliminating the other sibling, the one who threatened their individuality and wounded their narcissism and sense of omnipotence. In an expression of the *incestual* and *archaic fraternal complex*, each sibling unconsciously aspired to be the sole possessor of the maternal space of the nation-state and its phallus, and to take the place of the omnipotent father of the primitive horde. The formula became kill or be killed. According to Mitchell (2006, 2013a, 2013b, 2014), the 'law of the mother', which prohibited murder, was violated.

In this paradoxical environment, it became impossible for the brothers to live together under the same roof of the motherland, and yet it was fatal for them to separate (Caillot & Decherf, 1982). Through this conflict and through perverse, narcissistic and sadomasochistic manoeuvres, Lebanese siblings enacted the generational impossibility of separating and individuating from their conjoined neighbours. They denied their kinship and entertained a self-engendering phantasy. A group of Christian sons found it difficult to acknowledge Lebanon's Arab origins.

Syria may also have felt incomplete and expected its sibling, Lebanon, to provide magical reparation by becoming the part essential to its psychic survival. Lebanon was originally part of Greater Syria. In a state of *primary narcissism* and defence against castration, Syria apparently entertained the illusion of completeness. It perpetuated the myth of recovering Greater Syria

(Rabinovich, 1985)—an Arab kingdom with its capital in Damascus, once the seat of the Umayyad caliphs and the capital of the first Arab empire—by recovering the lost parts, namely, Palestine, Israel and Lebanon.

Syria denied the otherness of these nations and their right to be different. It recognised the right of the Maronites to maintain their autonomy in Mount Lebanon, but denied their right to a Greater Lebanon that included Syrian territories (Salibi, 1988). It also refused to demarcate the unclear segment of its border with Lebanon and Israel, and finally entered Lebanon in response to the call of the Lebanese Maronite president in 1976 to prevent the Lebanese leftist group and the PLO alliance from winning their war against the right wing, mainly Christian alliance. The call may have reflected Lebanon's difficulty in individuating itself, while the Syrian intervention expressed its desire to regain its lost part. Syria occupied Lebanon for almost 30 years, during which time it interfered in Lebanon's internal affairs.

The Palestinian siblings also refused to mourn their lost land and, according to some Christian sons, sought to replace it with Lebanese land in a war of substitution, thereby becoming involved in Lebanon's internal conflicts and fighting them as the embodiment of the Israelis (Tuawyni, as cited in Hudson, 1978). The fact that these Christian sons allied themselves with Israel, which armed, financed and directed them to fight the Palestinians, added to the confusion of identities.

Fraternal pacts

The pacts sealed by the Lebanese siblings were not based on the law or on the fundamental prohibitions of incest, cannibalism and murder. They repetitively enacted the pregenital functioning of the nation-state and the *archaic fraternal complex* of its members, resulting in the saga of the sibling murders.

The first Lebanese fraternal pact, designed by France in 1926 to establish the constitution of Lebanon as a nation-state, ensured the political supremacy of Lebanon's Christian allies. Moreover, according to the 1932 census (Salibi, 1988), the Maronites occupied most of the key positions in the new republic. In other words, this pact between the Lebanese brothers could be psychoanalytically interpreted as a manifestation of the primitive horde structure and the *archaic fraternal complex*. This situation eventually led to dissatisfaction and unrest among the Muslim brothers.

The Maronite Christian son found it difficult to mourn the old days and later the Mutasarrifate of Mount Lebanon, when his persecuted father took over sole rule of the area. He seems to have had difficulty in renouncing the unconscious desire to be the sole owner of the maternal space and the maternal phallus. Perhaps he carries the same fear of annihilation and entertains the phantasy of taking his father's place as ruler, excluding his rival Muslim siblings from equal rights and demanding sole rule over Greater Lebanon, since he believes he was the one who fought for its creation as a separate state, independent of Syria. He therefore felt betrayed when France, to maintain a viable state, forced him to share power with his Muslim sibling (Salibi, 1988).

With Lebanon's independence from the French mandate in 1943, the Lebanese Shiite, Sunnite and Maronite siblings drafted a national pact to lay the foundations of their country as a multi-confessional state. They agreed to consider Lebanon as a neutral, independent and sovereign country with an Arab character. The Maronite Christians agreed not to seek foreign intervention and to accept an Arab rather than a Western one, and the Muslims agreed to give up their aspirations to unite with Syria. It was as if the sons of the primitive Lebanese horde were trying to overcome their rivalry through this founding act. It was as if they had come together to symbolically kill and devour their French father, to put an end to the patriarchal horde and to establish a state of law in which they would live as brothers (Freud, 1913).

This National Pact, however, compulsively repeated the primitive horde structure and the *archaic fraternal complex*, confirming the inequality of the siblings under the pre-existing pact. The Maronites continued to aspire to occupy the privileged place of the admired and omnipotent father of the primitive horde and the unconscious desire to be the phallus of their mother nation and the exclusive owner of its womb. The National Pact gave the Maronite Christians a dominant role and a disproportionate amount of executive power (Krayem, 1997), eventually leading to the 1958 crisis between the Christian Maronites and their Muslim siblings. Although the crisis ended with the prime minister's slogan 'No Victor, No Vanquished', perhaps as an implicit recognition that sibling equality is necessary for the establishment of a state of law, the slogan did not find its way into the Lebanese constitution.

In 1969, the Lebanese army, to restore Lebanese sovereignty over its territory, attempted to liquidate the Palestinian commando that was using Lebanese territory to launch cross-border attacks against Israel. However, under pressure from Arab regimes that supported the presence of the Palestinian commandos in Lebanon, and in an effort to avoid splitting the country, Lebanon signed the Cairo Agreement (Salibi, 1976) with its Palestinian brothers, which authorised the armed presence of Palestinians in their camps and gave them the right to attack Israel across the Lebanese border, but with Lebanese consent. This pact further fragmented Lebanon by creating a Palestinian state within the Lebanese state.

Conflicts between the Lebanese army and Palestinian guerrillas continued. After its failed coup in Jordan in 1970, the PLO moved its base to Lebanon, polarising the country into camps of supporters and opponents. Christians and Palestinians continued to fight each other, and Israel raided Palestinian refugee camps in retaliation for cross-border guerrilla attacks. As internal stability deteriorated, the Lebanese and Palestinian siblings reached the Melkart Agreement in May 1973, whereby the PLO agreed to respect Lebanon's independence, stability and sovereignty in return for autonomy and the right to maintain its own militias in some Lebanese areas. This pact, unlike the previous one, did not preserve Lebanon's prerogative to exercise full authority over its territory in all circumstances (El-Khazen, 2000). Nor did it resolve the Lebanese-Palestinian conflict. Ultimately, the Lebanese siblings became more polarised and the civil war broke out in 1975.

The Syrians intervened in 1976 to stop the violence between the Lebanese siblings, but failed. Saudi Arabia, Syria, Egypt, Lebanon, the PLO and Kuwait met in Riyadh on 16 October 1976 and decided in a new pact to send an Arab Deterrent Force (ADF) to oversee the normalisation process (Rabinovich, 1985). The conference authorised PLO operations in Lebanon, albeit limited to the south, and allowed Syria to exercise political and military dominance over Lebanon. The relative stability and decline in violence that followed was, however, challenged by the assassination in 1977 of Druze leader Kamal Junblatt, who opposed Syria's presence and influence in Lebanon (O'Ballance, 1998).

Following the Israeli invasion of Lebanon in 1982, Operation Peace for Galilee, a Lebanese-Israeli pact was signed against the wishes of the Muslim Lebanese siblings. This new pact could not be sustained and could only re-enact the saga of the siblings' murders. Israel's ally, the elected president of Lebanon, was assassinated within days of his election. The American-brokered May 1983 pact between the Lebanese and Israeli governments was eventually abrogated under Syrian pressure and challenges from rival Lebanese factions (Eisenberg, 1997). Israel withdrew from southern Lebanon, except for a security belt controlled by its proxy, the South Lebanon Army (Chomski, 1983).

In 1983, the Lebanese siblings met in Geneva for a national dialogue conference. This produced few results other than an agreement on Lebanon's Arab identity. In 1984, the siblings met again in Lausanne, but their dialogue made no progress (Krayem, 1997). Finally, in an effort to end the civil war, a tripartite agreement was reached in Damascus in December 1985 between the dominant feuding sectarian siblings, namely, the Christian Lebanese Forces, the Shiite Amal Movement and the predominantly Druze Progressive Socialist Party. The agreement called for strategic integration in foreign policy and military matters for a reorganisation of the Lebanese state and society (Korn, 1986, p. 137). In other words, this fraternal pact was imbued with the archaic Lebanese and Syrian *archaic fraternal complex* and an unconscious desire to restore the original symbiotic state and a denial of the differences and individuality of each nation. It was annulled shortly afterwards.

In June 1987, the Prime Minister was assassinated and Lebanon abrogated the Cairo Agreement with the PLO. At the end of the president's term in 1988, Lebanon's executive power was divided and the legislative power was at stake (Krayem, 1997). In 1989, the Lebanese siblings reached a new national pact in Taif, Saudi Arabia, to end the civil war, define Lebanon's identity as Arab and reform its political structure based on the principle of mutual coexistence between the different sectarian groups and their proper political parliamentary representation (Krayem, 1997).

The Lebanese siblings did not seem to mourn their country as an idealised primitive horde to be ruled by one omnipotent father. They were unable to forge a fraternal pact based on the law and the renunciation of the direct realisation of destructive drive goals. They were unable to renounce the infantile desire to be the phallus of the mother nation-state and the exclusive owner of her womb, to finally gain access to a symbolic *fraternal complex* in which siblings are seen as equal and both similar and different, and thus to gain access to object investment.

When the Taif Agreement called for the disarmament of all national and non-national militias, it exempted the Shiite militia Hezbollah from this directive, instead allowing Hezbollah to remain armed in its capacity as a resistance force fighting Israel in the south. The pact between the sons of the primitive horde remained incomplete. Moreover, the implementation of this pact has given rise to a troika between the three Presidents of the Republic, the Council of Ministers and the Parliament (Krayem, 1997). Thus, despite the Taif Accord, Lebanon remained in a state of primitive horde, the country's ego remained fragile and its political and administrative institutions remained paralysed by sectarian divisions. In yet another compulsion to repeat, the president of Taif was assassinated within days of his election. Sectarian clashes erupted within the Maronite and Shiite Lebanese communities, and the Lebanese siblings continued to claim more than their share.

No fraternal pact was viable. Although the Lebanese siblings attempted to establish a state of law, they in fact re-enacted compulsively primitive orders in which the other brothers had to be eliminated. As a result, lawlessness continued.

Final remarks

In this chapter, I have reflected on Lebanon's history, its birth, its growth and its crises during its process of 'becoming'. An independent nation-state needs clear borders or a body envelope in which to construct itself; otherwise, its *psychic envelope* will fail to contain and transform the primitive, transgenerational, persecutory and annihilating anxieties of its nation-group and its citizens. I argued that Lebanon's difficulty in delineating its borders has left it in a state of confusion with its two neighbours and characterised its group psychic apparatus as a pregenital, narcissistic, *incestual* mode of family functioning. I also argued that Lebanese citizens were metaphorically part objects who, through their fraternal pacts, enacted the unconscious fratricidal phantasies of the *archaic fraternal complex*.

References

Bion, W. R. (1961). *Experiences in groups and other papers.* London: Tavistock. https://doi.org/10.4324/9780203359075

Caillot, J. P., & Decherf, G. (1982). *Thérapie Familiale Psychanalytique et Paradoxalité* [*Psychoanalytic family therapy and paradoxicality*]. Paris: Clancier-Guénaud.

Calame, J., & Charlesworth, E. (2011). *Divided cities: Belfast, Beirut, Jerusalem, Mostar and Nicosia.* Philadelphia: University of Pennsylvania Press.

Chomski, N. (1983). *The fateful triangle: The United States, Israel and the Palestinians.* Boston, MA: South End Press.

Eisenberg, L. Z. (1997). Israel's South Lebanon imbroglio. *Middle East Quarterly, 4*(2): 61–69.

El-Khazen, F. (2000). *The breakdown of the state in Lebanon, 1967–1976.* Cambridge, MA: Harvard University Press.

Eshel, D. (2001). The Israel–Lebanon border enigma. *IBRU Boundary and Security Bulletin, 8*(4): 72–83.

Falk, A. (1974). Border symbolism. *Psychoanalytic Quarterly, 43*(4): 650–660. https://doi.org/10.1080/21674086.1974.11926691

Freud, S. (1913). Totem and taboo. In: J. Strachey (Ed.), *The standard edition of the complete psychological works of Sigmund Freud, Volume XIII (1913–1914)* (pp. 7–162). London: The Hogarth Press.

Freud, S. (1914). On narcissism. In: J. Strachey (Ed.), *The standard edition of the complete psychological works of Sigmund Freud, Volume XIV (1914–1916): On the history of the psycho-analytic movement, papers on metapsychology and other works* (pp. 67–102). London: The Hogarth Press.

Freud, S. (1921). Group psychology and the analysis of the ego. In: J. Strachey (Ed.), *The standard edition of the complete psychological works of Sigmund Freud, Volume XVIII (1920–1922): Beyond the pleasure principle* (pp. 65–144). London: The Hogarth Press.

Hudson, M. C. (1978). The Palestinian factor in the Lebanese civil war. *Middle East Journal, 32*: 261–278.

Jaafar, R., & Stephan, M. J. (2009). Lebanon's independence intifada: How unarmed insurrection expelled Syrian forces. In: M. J. Stephan (Ed.), *Civilian Jihad: Nonviolent struggle, democratization, and governance in the Middle East* (p. 169). New York, NY: Palgrave Macmillan.

Jabbra, J. G., & Jabbra, N. W. (1983). Lebanon: Gateway to peace in the Middle East? *International Journal, 38*: 577–612. https://doi.org/10.2307/40202202

Kaës, R. (2008). *Le Complexe Fraternel [The fraternal complex].* Paris: Dunod.

Kaës, R. (2014). *Les Alliances Inconscientes [Unconscious alliances].* Paris: Dunod. https://doi.org/10.3917/dunod.kaes.2014.01

Kaës, R. (2016). *L'idéologie, l'idéal, l'idée, l'idole [The ideology, the ideal, the idea, the idol].* Paris: Dunod. https://doi.org/10.3917/dunod.kaese.2016.01

Kancyper, L. (2011). Exploring core concepts: Sexuality, dreams and the unconscious. *International Journal of Psychoanalysis, 92*(2): 265–267.

Klein, M. (1958). On the development of mental functioning. *International Journal of Psycho-Analysis, 39*(2–4): 84–90.

Korn, D. (1986). Syria and Lebanon: A fateful entanglement. *The World Today, 42*(8–9): 137–142.

Krayem, H. (1997). The Lebanese civil war and the Taif agreement. In: P. Salem (Ed.), *Conflict resolution in the Arab world, selected essays* (pp. 411–435). Beirut: AUB Publications.

Legorreta, G. (2013). Luis Kancyper. *Canadian Journal of Psychoanalysis, 21*(1): 193–201.

Lutsky, V. B. (1969). Chapter IX Lebanon, Syria and Palestine in the period of the Tanzimats (1840–70). (L. Nasser, Trans.). In: R. Daglish (Ed.), *Modern history of the Arab countries* (pp. 1–22). Moscow: Moscow for the USSR Academy of Sciences, Institute of the Peoples of Asia, Progress Publishers.

Mitchell, J. (2006). From infant to child: The sibling trauma, the rite de passage, and the construction of the "Other" in the social group. *Fort Da, 12*: 35–49.

Mitchell, J. (2013a). Siblings: Thinking theory. *Psychoanalytic Study of the Child, 67*: 14–34.

Mitchell, J. (2013b). The law of the mother: Sibling trauma and the brotherhood of war. *Canadian Journal of Psychoanalysis, 21*:145–159.

Mitchell, J. (2014). Siblings and the psychosocial. *Organizational and Social Dynamics, 14*: 1–12.

O'Ballance, E. (1998). *Civil war in Lebanon, 1975–1992*. New York, NY: St. Martin's Press Inc.

Rabinovich, I. (1985). *The war for Lebanon, 1970–1985*. Ithaca and London: Cornell University Press.

Racamier, P. C. (1992). *Le Génie des Origines [The genius of origins]*. Paris: Payot and Rivage.

Racamier, P. C. (1995). *L'inceste et l'incestuel [The incest and the incestual]*. Paris: Éditions du Collège.

Safa, O. (2006). Lebanon springs forward: Getting to Arab democracy. *Journal of Democracy, 17*(1): 22–37. https://doi.org/10.1353/jod.2006.0016

Salibi, K. S. (1976). *Cross roads to civil war: Lebanon 1958–1976*. Delmar, NY: Caravan Books.

Salibi, K. S. (1988). *A house of many mansions: The history of Lebanon reconsidered*. Berkeley: University of California Press.

Sella, A. (1986). Custodians and redeemers: Israeli leaders' perceptions of peace, 1967–79. *Middle Eastern Studies, 22*: 236–251. https://doi.org/10.1080/00263208608700661

Traboulsi, F. (2012). Greater Lebanon: The dialectics of attachment and detachment (1915–1920). In: F. Traboulsi (Ed.), *A history of modern Lebanon* (pp. 75–87). London: Pluto Press.

Volkan, V. D. (2004). *Blind trust: Large groups and their leaders in times of crisis and terror*. Charlottesville, VA: Pitchstone Publishing.

Chapter 3

Hezbollah
Lebanon's identified patient?

Hezbollah is the main representative of the Lebanese Shiite community and one of the most prominent political parties in Lebanon. In addition to being a major militant group and player in Lebanese politics, it is also involved in the dynamics of Middle Eastern politics and has influenced the recent history of the Arab world (Daher, 2019). Hezbollah's military wing has generated global polemics, and many countries have designated it, if not the entire overarching organisation, as a terrorist group. Today, Hezbollah is accused nationally and internationally of being the source of Lebanon's socio-economic and political crisis, which could threaten the Lebanese regime, if not downright efface Lebanon as a nation-state.

To analyse Hezbollah's role in Lebanese group dynamics, I will present an overview and psychoanalytical analysis of the history of Lebanon and the Lebanese Shiite community from which this political party emerged. In my interpretation of what Hezbollah has been doing to Lebanon and the Lebanese people, I will also address what it may unconsciously be doing for them, in the hope that this insight into Lebanon's unconscious dynamics may contribute to resolving the country's crises and Hezbollah's predicament. Moreover, the approach of this chapter may contribute to the understanding of ideological organisations in general.

I have argued, in Chapter 2, that Lebanon's struggle to build a viable independent state is related to its difficulty in doing the work of *primal mourning* (Racamier, 1992), which is a universal primal psychic process, by which the ego mourns its symbiosis with the mother and relinquishes total possession of the object. Its functioning was governed by *incestuality* (Racamier, 1995), which is a pregenital functioning that avoids intrapsychic conflicts and the work of primal mourning; it fights the desire to separate and individuate and maintains a confusion of boundaries between the Me and the not-Me. *Incestuality* has features of incest but without necessarily incestuous enactment. It is governed by the death drive and repetition compulsion. Primary process thinking and enactment characterise the functioning of groups and their constituent members.

Thus, in Chapter 2, I argued that Lebanon has difficulty mourning its symbiotic relationship with its neighbours. The blurred segments of Lebanon's

DOI: 10.4324/9781003545842-5

geographical boundaries or body envelope have created a perforated *psychic envelope* or *skin-ego* that has prevented it from adequately differentiating the Me from the not-Me. Lebanon's self has remained fragmented. Its parental functions—the maternal function of containment and the symbolic paternal function of establishing a post-Oedipal law that both forbids and protects—failed. Lebanon could not contain and symbolise the primitive transgenerational anxieties of its group and its citizens. The psychic bonds between Lebanon's sectarian communities broke down, and violent conflicts were unleashed between them. Lebanon's history has been marked by enactments that reflect its need to demarcate its borders and build a solid identity. Several internal (sectarian) and external (with Israel) wars followed.

Lebanon behaved like a dysfunctional family; its group apparatus expressed a paranoid-schizoid position (Klein, 1958) and a mobilised basic assumption mentality (Bion, 1961). The Lebanese people could not create a nation-state ego as a total object. Divided into sectarian subgroups, they were endowed as part objects with an infantile narcissistic power. Their loyalty was to the sectarian group, its idolised leader and its ideology; this loyalty contained them and provided them with a cohesive identity that compensated for their problematic Lebanese identity. The leader was cathected narcissistically, probably in a phallic defence against the fear of separation and individuation or castration anxiety and the recognition of kinship, thus sacrificing the institution of a symbolic order (Kaës, 2016).

In the light of the above analysis, and given Lebanon's perforated psychic envelope, its *incestual* dynamics and problematic individuation, I propose that Hezbollah, as one of Lebanon's children, has become the *designated patient* and symptom of the dysfunctional dynamics, complicated separation and individuation, and problematic loyalties of its large family nation-state after the 1989 Taif Accord. Hezbollah's *closing ideology* (Kaës, 2016), a paranoid vision of the world that excludes others and otherness as a response to misery and shame, may represent a generational denial of Lebanon's castration from the Ottoman Empire, its womb phantasy and avoidance of the work of *primal mourning*, and its problematic kinship with its newly defined territorial motherland among Lebanese sectarian communities. Like other sectarian communities, Hezbollah refers to its religious great-grandparents rather than to the motherland of its nation and its constitutional law of reason. Moreover, as a *designated patient*, Hezbollah can play the paradoxical role of scapegoat/messiah, with the dual function of holding its fragmented nation-state together and bearing the burden of being its breaking force (Houzel & Catoire, 1994).

An overview of the Shiite history in Lebanon

The Shiites arrived in Lebanon between the seventh and eleventh centuries. Persecuted by the Mamlukes, they emigrated to Jabal Āmil in southern

Lebanon and Baalbek in the northern Bekaa Valley. Between 1298 and 1305, the Mamlukes expelled the Shiites from Mount Lebanon, accusing them of conspiring against them. They were replaced by Maronite immigrants and Turkmen Sunnites. In the mid-eighteenth century, the Shiites were again attacked by local rulers, forcing them to evacuate the Lebanese coast as far south as the city of Sidon and retreat to the interior of the south and the northern Bekaa Valley.

With the creation of Greater Lebanon in 1920, the Shiites became a marginal community, both geographically and symbolically. The majority settled in the country's underdeveloped rural areas, far from the centres of political and economic power. From the time of Lebanon's independence from the French mandate in 1943 until 1974, the Shiites were relegated to a secondary position by the 1943 National Pact. They were also the last of the three Muslim groups (along with the Sunnites and Druze) to establish their own community institutions and manage their own community affairs. Until then, they had remained under the tutelage of the Sunnite community. Their political segregation was exacerbated by their poor socio-economic condition, and the Shiites were relegated to the lowest status within the national community. They made up the majority of Beirut's porters, waiters, newspaper sellers and shoeshine boys (Daher, 2019). In addition, Christians snubbed them because they were Muslims, and Muslims considered them the lowest among them. They were often referred to with the derogatory and humiliating term metwālīs, meaning uncouth and ignorant. The Lebanese religious communities promoted themselves defensively, strengthened their mutual alliances and repaired their loyalty to their groups and the nation-state, to the detriment of the Shiite community, whose narcissistic independence was discredited, denied, condemned and rejected. The Lebanese subgroups, in my opinion, enacted Lebanon's narcissistic struggle. The Shiites were scapegoated and unconsciously incited to play the role of martyrs (Boszormenyi-Nagy & Spark, 2013).

In sum, the Shiite history in Lebanon is one of successive traumas. Moreover, given that the majority of the Shiite community lives in the border areas of Lebanon, the perforated genealogical container of Lebanon (Benghozi, 2016) has added to their traumatic history and feelings of helplessness, shame and humiliation, leading to their *closing ideological position*. Moreover, the Shiite experience in Lebanon has apparently reactivated, through a time collapse, their previous generational chosen trauma (Volkan, 2009, 2013)—that of the martyrdom of the Prophet's grandson, Imam Hussein, in Karbala in AD 680 at the hands of the Umayyad Caliph Yazid. Typical of pathological mourning, the Lebanese Shiite group regressed; their 'traditional family values were replaced by ideologies' (Volkan & Fowler, 2009, p. 217). This regression is not limited to the Shiite community, but reflects, as I highlighted in Chapter 2, the *incestual* functioning of Lebanon, enacted through multiple internal sectarian ideologies and wars.

Hezbollah: the ideology

The first purely Shiite political mobilisation began in the 1970s, when Mūsā al-Sadr, a Lebanese Iranian philosopher and religious leader, won institutional independence for the Shiite community with the creation of a Supreme Shiite Council, approved by the Lebanese Parliament in 1967. The community then began to manage its own affairs. Later, al-Sadr established Harakat al-Mahrūmīn (the Movement of the Deprived) as the first Shiite militant structure to defend the rights of the poor and those neglected by the state (Daher, 2019; Norton, 2018). This helped to address the inferiority complex of the Shiite community. In 1973, al-Sadr founded the political and eventually paramilitary branch of this movement, the organisation Afwāj al-Muqāwama al-Lubnāniyya (the Lebanese Resistance Regiments), known by the acronym AMAL, which also means hope (Daher, 2019; Norton, 2018). The acronym, in my view, carries the roots of the paradoxical scapegoat/messiah role of the Shiite, and ultimately Hezbollah, in the Lebanese nation-state. By failing to defend its people in the south and to adequately guarantee their socio-economic rights, Lebanon may have implicitly delegated its role to the AMAL of the Shiite community and eventually to Hezbollah. In January 1975, following several Israeli attacks on southern Lebanon, al-Sadr called on the Lebanese people to form an armed resistance force. The AMAL and Palestinian refugee fighters began their joint operations in the area.

Al-Sadr's disappearance in 1978 traumatised the Shiite community, which refused to contemplate his death and spoke instead of an occultation. His absence changed the sociopolitical trajectory of the community and led to the creation of Hezbollah. Moreover, the success of the Iranian revolution in 1979 symbolically broke the curse that had previously contaminated sociopolitical relations for Lebanese Shiites (Daher, 2019).

In March 1978, Israel invaded southern Lebanon in response to Palestinian guerrilla cross-border raids from that area and established a security zone on its northern border. Its second invasion of southern Lebanon in June 1982 mobilised the Shiite desire to fight the invaders, which translated into a localised military organisation, the Islamic Resistance in Lebanon (IRL), whose mission was to fight (muhimma jihādiyya) to end the Israeli occupation. Thus, after Israel withdrew from most of southern Lebanon in 1985 and continued to occupy an area on the border as a security zone, the IRL used this area to launch its attacks. In other words, Lebanon's difficulty in demarcating and defending its borders unconsciously incited the Shiites to take on this responsibility.

In May 1984, the network of institutions attached to the IRL adopted the name *Hizb Allāh* (Hezbollah), or the Party of God, in reference to the Koran, which states that the party of God will know bliss and be victorious. *Hizb Allāh* is therefore the party loyal to God, as opposed to *Hizb al-Shaytān*, the party of the devil, which consists of evil people. Thus, a paranoid-schizoid

Shiite ideology could have developed, not only as a reaction to the community's traumatic experiences and feelings of shame and humiliation but also as an enactment of Lebanon's fragile ego state, its psychotic group dynamics and its problematic individuation and loyalty. The Lebanese Messiah could have arisen to help Lebanon define its bodily envelope that distinguishes the Me from the not-Me.

Hezbollah officially declared its presence on 16 February 1985. Although it affirmed its commitment to Islamic unity, its philosophy included fewer Islamist paradigms and expressed more pragmatic, communitarian aspirations for a strong and just state. Unlike the Lebanese state, Hezbollah proclaimed that it would protect the Shiite community in the South against Israeli aggressions, and unlike the sectarian system, it aimed to meet the community's socio-economic needs. The Shiites in Lebanon perceive Hezbollah to be a political movement and an organisation that provides them with social services that are mostly missing from their areas. However, Hezbollah's social institutions aim to defuse resentment that could jeopardise the Lebanese public's support—particularly the Shiites—for the IRL and prevent an opposing home front from emerging (Daher, 2019). Through these social institutions, Hezbollah attempted to build a Shiite identity as an active volunteer in reparation of the deprived and inferior Shiite image.

However, Hezbollah's identity and kinship remain problematic. Hezbollah is a hybrid of ideological and cultural roots. Although it argues that its loyalty remains to its homeland and the interests of its homeland, this is challenged by the fact that for political leadership it adheres to the *wilāyat al-faqīh* (the guardianship of the Islamic jurist) in Iran. Despite its freedom of decision and action, its allegiance remains to the Waliy, or guardian, as the Guide of the Revolution who plays the dual role of religious and political authority (Daher, 2019; Norton, 2018). Hezbollah's ideology thus expresses Lebanon's conflicting loyalties. Hezbollah's Lebanese siblings have denounced this loyalty as evidence of its non-Lebanese character, accusing it of being an Iranian agent in Lebanon. Through Hezbollah's ideology and the conflict over its allegiance, Lebanon enacted its problematic kinship.

Hezbollah: the scapegoat/messiah

From 1984, the IRL began carrying out operations under its own name to liberate southern Lebanon from Israeli occupation. Hezbollah referred to these operations as martyrdom operations. In Hezbollah parlance, dying as a martyr is a courageous and selfless act that is the ultimate manifestation of sacrifice. The candidate for martyrdom in Hezbollah ideology upholds the sacrificial account of the Prophet's grandson Hussein as their ideal and wishes to replicate it. Benslama (2014) emphasised the persecutory nature of an ideal father who demands the repetition of Hussein's sacrifice and his revenge. The candidate for martyrdom serves as an intercessor between God and the members of his community, whose shame and guilt he purifies through his acts of sacrifice and revenge, which are acts demanded by God. By imitating Hussein's call to martyrdom, revolutionary Shiites identify with Hussein and transform their feelings of guilt into pride.

Thus, Hezbollah's unconscious mission seemed to carry the burden of both its community's traumatic history and Lebanon's difficulty in demarcating its geographical borders to individuate, establish a solid identity and resolve its problematic generational loyalties. However, its role remained paradoxical and spoke to Lebanon's difficulty in individuating itself. While Hezbollah fights Israel on Lebanon's southern border, it refuses to demarcate its northern and eastern borders with Syria and maintains illegal crossings used by smugglers, with devastating consequences for the country's security and economy. In this way, Hezbollah may be enacting the Lebanese generational phantasy of returning to the womb of mother Syria.

Between 1982 and 1986, despite its denials, Hezbollah was accused of being involved in or linked to suicide bombings targeting American, French and Israeli troops in Lebanon. Since 1990, Hezbollah has also been accused of terrorism against civilians and diplomats in various parts of the world in the service of Tehran (Daher, 2019). Hezbollah has apparently become the scapegoat that tyrannises its nation-state and Lebanese sibling sectarian subgroups, its omnipotence enacting Lebanon's lack of clearly defined borders.

With the end of the civil war in Lebanon, by virtue of the 1989 Taif Agreement, the Lebanese sectarian groups laid down their arms but authorised the IRL to keep its own weapons to fight the occupation forces in the South. Some factions even donated their weapons to Hezbollah to help it fulfil its mission. The IRL would defend Lebanese territory militarily and was supported politically and diplomatically by the Lebanese government, both domestically and internationally (Daher, 2019). In other words, through the Taif Accord, Lebanon's warring factions stopped militarily and legally empowering Hezbollah to protect their large family nation-state, unconsciously delegating the organisation to demarcate its borders with neighbouring countries and complete the process of separation-individuation. This delegation was further consolidated by the 2006 Mar Mikhael Memorandum of Understanding between the Free Patriotic Party and Hezbollah. As an offensive alliance (Kaës, 2014), sealed to fulfil a project or to attack and dominate the other siblings, the Memorandum provided Hezbollah with a Christian cover and thus influenced Lebanese politics. Lebanon functioned with the basic assumption mentality pairing (Bion, 1961), acting as if its survival depended on these two parties producing a magical solution to its difficulties. However, instead of structuring Lebanon's group life, the unconscious alliances siblings became alienating (Kaës, 2014).

The Taif delegation questioned the nature of the relationship between the Lebanese government and Hezbollah. This agreement was reminiscent of the 1969 Cairo Agreement between representatives of the Lebanese government and the Palestine Liberation Organisation (PLO), which allowed the

Palestinian guerrillas to keep their weapons in their refugee camps and, with Lebanese consent, to fight Israel across the Lebanese border (Salibi, 1976). Both the Cairo and Taif Pacts expressed the fragmentation of Lebanon; both established a state within the Lebanese state. Moreover, the Memorandum of Understanding has been accused of being at the root of Lebanon's current socio-economic and political crises, which threatens its existence as a nation-state: Had it not been for the Christian cover given to Hezbollah, the latter would not have gained its current grip on Lebanese affairs.

Thus, the unconscious Lebanese delegation maintained the Shiite loyalty problem without resolution, which eventually led to Hezbollah's misuse of arms, power conflicts and relational stagnation (Boszormenyi-Nagy & Spark, 2013) among the Lebanese sectarian communities. Hezbollah, as the *designated patient* that ensures the internal balance of its family, became a persecutory object that threatened Lebanon and had to be simultaneously repulsed and preserved by the other Lebanese sectarian siblings. In the pathological dynamics of Lebanon, Hezbollah and its military wing, the IRL, instead of elaborating the phantasics that it arouses as a persecutory object, have apparently become the scapegoat that terrorises its family group by virtue of the Taif Agreement.

Beginning in the late 1990s, Hezbollah evolved from an Iranian-sponsored extremist group that refused to participate in Lebanese politics to a political party that integrated itself into the Lebanese Parliament and government (Norton, 2018). It worked to convey that it was a national and moderate party that promoted interfaith peace, emphasising its non-antisemitic perspective and the political and ideological nature of its aversion for the State of Israel (Daher, 2019). However, the 1990s also saw the resumption of IRL attacks against the Israeli occupier in southern Lebanon, which led to Israel's Operation Grapes of Wrath on 11 April 1996 and the massacres in the village of Qana. For the Shiite, time collapsed and the present collided with the past (Volkan, 2013). Qana became 'the Karbala of the twentieth century' (Norton, 2018, p. 73), and Israel became the Umayyad ruler, Caliph Yazid, who had martyred Imam Hussein. This time, however, the Shiite, having learned from Karbala, confronted and defeated the embodiment of Yazid (Norton, 2018). The subsequent ceasefire agreement officially recognised the IRL's right to defend itself against the Israeli army. Hezbollah's image changed from that of a terrorist organisation to that of a resistance force legitimised by the international community. It became the only Arab force since 1967 capable of defeating the Israeli army and damaging its armour enough to affect its domestic politics. Once again, Hezbollah became the messiah who would save Lebanon, if not the entire Arab world, from its enemies.

In 2000, with the liberation of South Lebanon from the Israeli occupation, the Shiites finally felt recognised. Hezbollah was praised by most of the Lebanese political class, as well as the leaders of Arab countries, who spoke of the restoration of Arab pride. The Shiites felt that the liberation was their baptism into national identity and history (Daher, 2019, p. 292); they had paid the price in blood. Their communal inferiority complex and feelings of shame and humiliation seemed to be finally repaired. However, Hezbollah's messianic role eventually reverted to that of a scapegoat.

After the attacks of 11 September 2001, the neoconservative American administration listed Hezbollah as a terrorist organisation. Although Lebanon rejected the designation, the Cedar Revolution of 2005, which drove Syrian forces out of Lebanon, divided the Lebanese. The March 14 anti-Syrian Alliance described the Cedar Revolution as the second independence, after the independence from the French mandate in 1943. With this classification, Hezbollah and the Shiites felt that 14 March had disqualified the IRL's achievements in ending the Israeli occupation in 2000. For them, the Israeli withdrawal in 2000 should have been considered the second independence and the Cedar Revolution against the Syrian presence the third independence. They realised that their sacrifices in South Lebanon did not improve their image in the eyes of their siblings—they remained the shoeshine boys (Daher, 2019). Moreover, some March 14 partisans also called for the disarmament of the IRL, and Hezbollah felt that it had to deal with an internal enemy in addition to the external one.

As the euphoria of the Israeli withdrawal began to fade, so did the idolisation of Hezbollah. Hezbollah's opponents claimed that the organisation's repeated attacks on Israel, even when limited to disputed border areas, were irresponsible and unjustified (Norton, 2018). When Hezbollah announced the capture of Israeli soldiers in 2006, the Lebanese cabinet denied knowledge of and responsibility for the operation. Many Lebanese factions believed that the IRL was directed by Syria and/or Iran. Western governments shared this view and reiterated the need to disarm the militias in Lebanon. The capture of the Israeli soldiers triggered a war with Israel that lasted 33 days and had a devastating impact on Lebanon's infrastructure and economy. At the end of the 2006 Lebanon War, Hezbollah, expressing the omnipotence inherent in its ideology, celebrated its divine victory and the public saw it as God's direct intervention in the IRL's strength. God supposedly protected the IRL during the battles, and the Imāms descended from heaven to support the fighters. The fighters of 2006 became the men of God, in contrast to the human martyrs of 2000, who were lauded as courageous yet humble (Daher, 2019).

In contrast to the Arab world's celebration of Hezbollah's victory, the idolisation of Hezbollah was contested within Lebanon (Norton, 2018). On 14 March, a national campaign against Hezbollah and the IRL's weapons began, leading to UN Security Council Resolution 1701 (Daher, 2019). The 2006 Lebanon War also ushered in a new relationship between the Shiite and the other Lebanese religious communities. No longer having to prove their Lebanese identity, the Shiites reversed their stigma and healed their sense of subjugation. From pseudo-Lebanese, they became the super-Lebanese who had sacrificed the most for their country (Daher, 2019). The Shiite community placed itself at the centre of Lebanon's creation, summarising Lebanon's history as a long tradition of resistance to occupation and oppression.

Moreover, the 2006 Lebanon War ushered in a new phase in Lebanese sociopolitical life, in which rancour, polarisation and obstruction prevailed. The radicals of the March 14 Alliance discredited the idea of a Lebanese victory over Israel and accused Hezbollah of being a state within a state, calling on the Lebanese state to extend its sovereignty to the entire country. They described Hezbollah as a mafia and a terrorist organisation subservient to Tehran, accusing it of plotting to overthrow the Lebanese regime and change the nation's identity. Eventually, this negative attitude extended to the Shiite community as a whole; it did not belong to the Lebanese identity and was a danger to it. The March 14 Alliance characterised Shiite dogma as a culture of death to describe Hezbollah's love of war and martyrdom, while it described its own existential values as a culture of life, a normal life.

Hezbollah rejected these accusations and refused to disarm, arguing that the IRL had to defend Lebanon as long as the army could not (Daher, 2019). Metaphorically, Hezbollah became Lebanon's messiah. The Hezbollah camp accused the majority of treason and collaboration with the United States and Israel, of renouncing national sovereignty and taking orders from Washington, Tel Aviv and Riyadh. The martyr role, which mitigated Hezbollah's guilt for past, present or future disloyalty, empowered it to hold others accountable. As a result, Lebanon appears to be engaged in a guilt-driven system in which each Lebanese community feels guilty for what it has done to the other communities over generations of sectarian civil wars and massacres. In such a system, Hezbollah felt the least burdened by guilt and thus felt endowed with 'the strongest monitoring position as the controller of the others' guilt feelings' (Boszormenyi-Nagy & Spark, 2013, p. 127). Thus, each group continued to defensively promote itself at the expense of the other groups in a generational repetition compulsion. Each group identified with the victim position, projecting onto others the denied parts of the self, internal objects and intolerable affect. In other words, as is typical of *incestual* dynamics, Lebanon dealt with its archaic separation anxieties at the expense of paranoid-schizoid splitting (Klein, 1958).

This paranoid-schizoid mentality resurfaced when the International Criminal Court, which was to investigate assassinations in Lebanon—including that of Prime Minister Rafik Hariri—pointed to Hezbollah's possible involvement. Lebanon's long political crisis culminated in the bloody events of May 2008 in West Beirut, which almost sparked a new civil war in the country. The interpretation of the events took on an existential dimension, threatening the future of Lebanon and its identity. The March 14 Alliance demonised Hezbollah, accusing it of invading the capital and turning its weapons inwards. Hezbollah, in turn, felt further alienated from Lebanese identity. The public in the IRL reinforced the image of a protective Hezbollah that had prevented a national massacre. For its public, Hezbollah became the guardian of the nation against both external aggression and internal threats.

Thus, as Lebanon's *identified patient*, Hezbollah continued to oscillate between the paradoxical roles of scapegoat, source of the nation's suffering and messiah, maintaining the family's fragile solidarity and enabling its psychological survival by shouldering the burden of its conflicts. To end the sectarian violence and the 18-month political stalemate, the Lebanese siblings signed the Doha Agreement, another fraternal pact that provided for the formation of a national unity government and gave the Hezbollah-led opposition veto power (Immigration and Refugee Board of Canada Lebanon, 2008; Worth & Bakri, 2008). This fraternal pact, which shifted power to Hezbollah and its allies, reiterated previous pacts and reaffirmed the primitive horde state. It also expressed Lebanon's paradoxical attitude towards Hezbollah; Lebanon rejects Hezbollah's actions and yet continues to delegate it to carry out its mission.

With the outbreak of the anti-Assad rebellion in Syria in 2011, the IRL sided with the regular Syrian army and intervened in Syria's internal political dynamics, allegedly to defend Lebanon from jihadi attacks on its border. The IRL's involvement in Syria eventually led the European Union to designate the party's military wing as a terrorist organisation in July 2013 (Daher, 2019; Norton, 2018). This decision added to Hezbollah's ostracism, which was further exacerbated when the Gulf Cooperation Council and most members of the Arab League denounced Hezbollah as a terrorist group (Norton, 2018). Thus, in an act of omnipotence and an unconscious search for boundaries, Hezbollah's tyranny spread beyond the borders of its nuclear family, Lebanon, to its extended family of Middle Eastern and Arab nation-states, and eventually to international family of nation-states. In their condemnation, the Arab and international states had to set limits for Hezbollah and its nation-state.

Following Lebanon's recent economic collapse, the international community stepped in to save the country from total collapse. Under pressure, Hezbollah initiated UN-sponsored talks with Israel to demarcate the disputed maritime borders. Again, by initiating these talks while continuing to interfere in Syria's internal affairs, Hezbollah enacted Lebanon's historically paradoxical stance of separation and individuation.

In October 2019, civil protests broke out in Lebanon, as a reaction to sectarian rule, a stagnant economy, corruption and the government's failure to secure fundamental services. However, although these protests attracted demonstrators from all religious sects, Hezbollah saw them as a foreign conspiracy against Shiites and mobilised with its ally, AMAL, to protect the status quo and smother the uprising (Yee & Saad, 2020), repeatedly invading protest sites and attacking protesters. Although Hezbollah and AMAL did not openly encourage these attacks, the men who infiltrated the protests shouted party slogans or 'Shiites! Shiites!' Hezbollah, Lebanon's *identified patient* and symptom of Lebanon's pathological large family-group dynamics, continues to tyrannise its family nation-state. By virtue of the Taif Agreement of

1989, its authority legitimised the use of its weapons to protect its nation-state against foreign aggression and occupation, which turned into an abuse of power during sectarian conflicts.

Hassan Nasrallah: the idol

To gain a sense of security and regain its *primary narcissism* (Freud, 1914), the regressed Shiite group pledged allegiance to Hezbollah and its leaders. It functioned under the aegis of basic assumption mentalities of dependency (Bion, 1961) and incohesion-massification as a fused and confused mass (Hopper 2009; Hopper and Weinberg, 2018). The Shiite group, like the other Lebanese sectarian groups, thus organised itself around the idealisation of its ideological party and its leaders, as well as identification with both leaders and group members. Massification group mentality often reflects a desire to merge with a maternal, imagined spirit and body (Hopper, 2009).

For Lebanese Shiites, Hezbollah seems to have become an idealised containing mother figure or 'good breast', repairing their narcissistic injuries (Chasseguet-Smirgel, 1985). Hassan Nasrallah, Hezbollah's third secretary-general, became the object of their idealised projections. In this way, the omnipotent idea, the tyrannical ideal and the seductive power of the idol become intertwined (Kaës, 2016). The figure of the tyrant, a self-proclaimed pseudo-father, substituted the symbolic function of the father. Hassan Nasrallah, as a leader, became a remnant of the primal father. Hassan Nasrallah became the leader of an organisation that could destabilise Israel's political class by 'having it rejected in its own country' (Daher, 2019, p. 151).

Since his appointment as Secretary-General of Hezbollah in 1992, Nasrallah has personified the organisation's legitimacy and cooperation on the national front. In September 1997, with the death of his eldest son in battle on the southern front, Nasrallah's idolised image acquired a human dimension that further connected him to his admirers and strengthened his credibility as a leader. Nasrallah's reaction and attitude to the event endowed him with a divine quality and transformed him into a living legend in the eyes of the Shiite community (Daher, 2019). By sacrificing his son to wage his war, he metaphorically became Abraham, the primal father who offered his son to God.

With the liberation of southern Lebanon in 2000, Nasrallah became not only a hero in Lebanon, the Arab world and, to some extent, the Muslim world, but also one of the most charismatic men in history. The grudging respect of party opponents fed the pride of the Shiite community in having someone of Nasrallah's stature at the head of their community. He proved to be a great strategist who, unlike those who had called for diplomatic negotiations with Israel in the 1990s, knew that only an armed solution would succeed.

During the 2006 Lebanon War, Nasrallah became the main guarantor of his organisation's mobilisation strength. The image of a visionary leader who is never wrong, coupled with the IRL's military effectiveness, including surreal victories in several battles, added a new superhuman facet to the Nasrallah persona. Although not exactly seen as the Messiah who must return to restore justice on earth, Nasrallah's public saw him as the harbinger of return of the Mahdī (the end-times divine saviour) (Daher, 2019). He became semi-divine and shared the infallible quality of the Imāms. He became Hussein's infant son, Ali Zayn al-Abidin, the sole survivor of the Karbala tragedy, who would carry on the imamate as the successor of the Prophet Muhammad (Norton, 2018).

In Damascus, the 2006 Lebanon War reactivated the chosen glory (Volkan, 2013) of liberating Jerusalem from the Crusaders in 1187: 'Nasrallah was celebrated as a modern-day Salah al-Din (Saladin), the Kurdish general hero for this liberation' (Norton, 2018, p. 131). He was blindly trusted in all areas and seen as the one 'who says what he does and does what he says' (Daher, 2019, p. 305). The Israeli press reinforced Nasrallah's oracular image by suggesting that the Israelis found Hezbollah's secretary-general more reliable than their own leaders. The Shiites were proud of this recognition, which compensated for their feelings of shame and humiliation. Indeed, in a speech in August 2006, Nasrallah addressed the Shiites' feelings of shame and promised his community that they would never be taken back to their shoeshine days (Daher, 2019). However, when Nasrallah sided with the Syrian regime against the anti-Assad uprising in 2011, calling for an end to violence in favour of a negotiated settlement, his image as a pan-Arab hero was severely tarnished. Thus, the idol Hassan Nasrallah, like the organisation he leads, oscillates between the two sides of the same coin: the inhuman image of the Messiah/Mahdi and the scapegoat/demon.

Final remarks

Hezbollah appears to have borne the brunt of Lebanon's difficulties after the 1989 Taif Accord; all Lebanese sectarian groups continue to maintain the ideological, political and sectarian primitive horde mentality that idolises their primal father-leader, even if not militarily like Hezbollah. The subgroups, through their actions and alliances, directly or indirectly contribute to the prevailing state of corruption and perverse use of the law, which poses a threat to Lebanon's viability as a nation-state. These pathological dynamics led to the October 2019 uprising, which demanded the overthrow of all political leaders.

References

Benghozi, P. (2016). Clinique identitaire de la radicalisation idéologique et Djihad dans les organisations incestueuses et incestuelles [An identity-based clinical approach to ideological radicalisation in incestuous and incestual organisations]. *Revue de Psychothérapie Psychanalytique de Groupe*, *67*(2): 51–66.

Benslama, F. (2014). *La Guerre des Subjectivités en Islam [The war of subjectivities in Islam]*. Paris: Éditions Lignes.

Bion, W. R. (1961). *Experiences in groups and other papers*. London: Tavistock. https://doi.org/10.4324/9780203359075

Boszormenyi-Nagy, I., & Spark, G. M. (2013). *Invisible loyalties*. London & New York: Routledge.

Chasseguet-Smirgel, J. (1985). The ego ideal and the psychology of groups. *Free Associations 1, 2*: 31–60.

Daher, A. (2019). *Hezbollah: Mobilization and power*. New York, NY: Oxford University Press.

Freud, S. (1914). On narcissism. In: J. Strachey (Ed.), *The standard edition of the complete psychological works of Sigmund Freud, Volume XIV (1914–1916): On the history of the psycho-analytic movement, papers on metapsychology and other works* (pp. 67–102). London: The Hogarth Press.

Hopper, E. (2009). The theory of the basic assumption of incohesion: Aggregation/massification or (BA) I: A/M. *British Journal of Psychotherapy, 25*: 214–229.

Hopper, E., & Weinberg, H. (2018). *The social unconscious in persons, groups and societies: Mainly theory*. The new international library of group analysis book (Kindle edition., Vol. 1). London & New York: Routledge.

Houzel, D., & Catoire, G. (1994). *La Famille comme Institution [The family as an institution]*. Paris: Apsygée.

Immigration and Refugee Board of Canada, Lebanon. (2008). *Overall political conditions in 2008*. Retrieved from https://www.refworld.org/docid/49913b61c.html

Kaës, R. (2014). *Les Alliances Inconscientes [Unconscious alliances]*. Paris: Dunod. https://doi.org/10.3917/dunod.kaes.2014.01

Kaës, R. (2016). *L'idéologie, l'idéal, l'idée, l'idole [The ideology, the ideal, the idea, the idol]*. Paris: Dunod. https://doi.org/10.3917/dunod.kaese.2016.01

Klein, M. (1958). On the development of mental functioning. *International Journal of Psycho-Analysis, 39*(2–4): 84–90.

Norton, A. R. (2018). *Hezbollah*. Princeton, NJ: Princeton University Press.

Racamier, P. C. (1992). *Le Génie des Origines [The genius of origins]*. Paris: Payot and Rivage.

Racamier, P. C. (1995). *L'inceste et l'incestuel [The incest and the incestual]*. Paris: Éditions du Collège.

Salibi, K. S. (1976). *Cross roads to civil war: Lebanon 1958–1976*. Delmar, NY: Caravan Books.

Volkan, V. D. (2009). Large-group identity, international relations and psychoanalysis. *International Forum of Psychoanalysis, 18*(4): 206–213. https://doi.org/10.1080/08037060902727795

Volkan, V. D. (2013). Large-group-psychology in its own right: Large-group identity and peace-making. *International Journal of Applied Psychoanalytic Studies, 10*(3): 210–246. https://doi.org/10.1002/aps.1368

Volkan, V. D., & Fowler, J. C. (2009). Large-group narcissism and political leaders with narcissistic personality organization. *Psychiatric Annals, 39*(4): 214–222. https://doi.org/10.3928/00485713-20090401-09

Worth, R. F., & Bakri, N. (2008). Deal for Lebanese factions leaves Hezbollah stronger. *The New York Times*. Retrieved from https://www.nytimes.com/2008/05/22/world/middleeast/22lebanon.html

Yee, V., & Saad, H. (2020). For Lebanon's Shiites, a dilemma: Stay loyal to Hezbollah or keep protesting? *The New York Times*. Retrieved from https://www.nytimes.com/2020/02/04/world/middleeast/lebanon-protests-shiites-hezbollah.html

Chapter 4

Israeli-Palestinian conflict
The *archaic fraternal complex*

A brief historical overview

In biblical times, Palestine referred to the region of Canaan—the area between the Mediterranean Sea and the Jordan River. The cradle of Judaism and Christianity, Palestine has been referred to variously as the Jewish Land of Israel, the Christian Holy Land and the Arabic Filastin. Strategically located between three continents and a religious, cultural, commercial and political crossroads, Palestine's history has been turbulent, with many kingdoms and powers ruling over it. It has not been an autonomous state since the time of the Crusades, and its geographical borders are constantly being redefined (Biger, 1981, 2008).

In 1516, the Ottoman Empire conquered Palestine and ruled for four centuries over Bilad el-Cham (the countries of Damascus), which included modern-day Syria, Lebanon, Jordan, Israel and Palestine. The Ottomans, who usually named their administrative provinces after the capitals of the Empire, did not officially use the appellation Palestine, but it remained popular (Gerber, 1998). For the Ottomans, Filastin referred to the Holy Land rather than a specific territory (Lewis, 1980). They did not recognise it as a separate administrative subdivision, nor did they clearly delineate its borders (Biger, 1981, 2008). From 1840 onwards, Palestine referred to the Western consular jurisdictions (Kark, 1994), or to the region extending north-south, usually from Rafah to the Litani River, now part of Lebanon. Palestine's western border was the sea. However, the demarcation of its eastern border remained unclear (Biger, 1981, 2008). In 1873, the administrative reorganisation that lasted until 1914 divided Palestine into three main parts, with the borders of the southern part remaining unclear (Biger, 2008; Porath, 1974). For the Arabs, Filastin at this time referred either to all of Palestine or to the Jerusalem Sanjaq (Porath, 1974) and Ramla (Gerber, 1998).

In 1867, the southern half of Palestine was separated from the Syrian province to become directly accountable to the Sultan (Biger, 2008; Ramzy et al., 2007). This sparked the separation from the other sibling districts in the region. However, there was no open conflict between Jews and Muslims in Jerusalem, even though the Palestinian identity originated in this area and civil

DOI: 10.4324/9781003545842-6

wars took place in Syria; Jews and Muslims united against external enemies (Ramzy et al., 2007).

By the end of 1917, Britain had conquered Palestine. Meanwhile, to gain the support of the various groups in the Middle East, Britain concluded several conflicting and overlapping agreements with both Arabs and Jews over land ownership. These agreements created confusion over ownership and consequently national identity, setting the stage for the problems of the twentieth century (Brenner, 2009). In the 1915 McMahon-Hussein Agreement, Britain pledged to recognise Arab independence after the war and promised much of the land to the Arabs in return for their support in the rebellion against the Ottoman Empire and assistance in expelling the Turks. However, the Sykes-Picot Agreement of 1916 demarcated the post-First World War borders of the Middle East, placing the Arab provinces of the Empire under British or French tutelage, and with the Balfour Declaration of 1917, the British government supported 'a Jewish national home in Palestine' (Brenner, 2009, p. 64).

On 20 March 1920, a Syrian congress at Damascus rejected the Balfour Declaration and elected Faysal I, king of a united Syria, including Palestine. This decision echoed that of the first Palestinian Arab Conference of Muslim-Christian Associations held in Jerusalem in February 1919. However, in April 1920, at the San Remo Conference, the League of Nations, ceded Ottoman Palestine to Britain, including present-day Israel and Jordan. By July 1920, the French had deposed King Faysal, shattering the dream of founding an independent Arab Palestine within a federated Syrian state. To the Palestinian Arabs, 1920 was 'ām al-nakbah, the year of catastrophe'.

Violent clashes between Jews and Arabs occurred throughout the 1920s and 1930s, leading to the Wailing Wall Riots of 1929, a turning point in the history of Jewish-Arab relationship. After these riots, Arabs no longer differentiated Jews of Arab origin from those of Eastern European origin, instead of considering them as a unified group with identical national goals. Meanwhile, Jews came to the conclusion that a Jewish state had to be established. British policy also shifted towards the Zionist lobby and the Balfour Declaration.

In 1936, an economic crisis caused by mass Jewish immigration and land purchases led to another major Arab revolt. In 1937, a Peel Commission inquiry into the conflict concluded that Palestine contained two cultures with conflicting political aspirations, necessitating a partition of the land. However, the Arab Higher Committee rejected the Peel recommendations and another uprising broke out, leading the mandate government to dissolve the Arab Higher Committee and declare it illegal. In addition, the British government issued the White Paper of 1939, which stated that Palestine must become a bi-national state for Arabs and Jews. It also restricted Jewish immigration to Palestine by requiring Arab consent to immigration and restricting Jewish land purchases. However, illegal immigration into Palestine continued until the end of British rule.

On 29 November 1947, the United Nations (UN) General Assembly decreed the partition of Palestine; Britain terminated its Mandate for Palestine, effective 15 May 1948; and on 14 May 1948, the State of Israel declared its independence. Following the 1947 UN resolution, the Arab-Israeli War broke out in 1948. The Israelis interpreted this war as a War of Independence they had fought and won, whereas the Palestinians construed it as *Al-Nakba* or *the Catastrophe*.

The essence of Israeli-Palestinian discord is, in the words of Jarrar (2010), 'a protest against a postmodern colonialist project to create an exclusive national entity for the Jewish people by eliminating and replacing the existence of Palestine' (p. 198). Thus, although the apparent cause of contemporary Arab and Muslim hostility towards Jews appears to be religious, Ostow (2007) argues that it stems from the creation of the State of Israel on Muslim Arab territory in 1948. For the author, much of the conflict before that was based on the Zionist movement, which sought to establish a Jewish state in the land the Romans called Palestine to escape a long history of European persecution, oppression and anti-Semitism. The emergence of the Zionist movement, and its encouragement by the Balfour Declaration, intensified Arab-Jewish rivalry. Stora and Meddeb (2013) argue that the central events that caused the separation of Arabs and Jews were the Second World War, the Holocaust, the establishment of the State of Israel in 1948 and the Palestinian exodus, as well as the subsequent Arab-Israeli wars, such as the Suez Expedition and the Six-Day War. In addition, after the establishment of the State of Israel and the subsequent Arab-Israeli wars, anti-Semitic policies led to an exodus of Mizrahi or Oriental Jews from the Arab countries where they had lived (Beker, 2005). Oriental Jews were either expelled or chose to flee, most of them emigrating to Israel. The Palestinian and Mizrahi exoduses led to a population exchange in the Middle East.

I argue that the Israeli-Palestinian discord may be symptomatic of problematic unconscious dynamics of separation and individuation. In envisaging the creation of an independent nation-state at the expense of denying the history, identity and rights of the indigenous people, the Zionist liberation movement that emerged in Central and Eastern Europe in the late nineteenth century expressed these problematic dynamics among the Jewish people. Moreover, after the dissolution of the Ottoman Empire, the Arab-Palestinian and Jewish peoples differed in their desire to build independent nation-states.

A group and family psychoanalytic interpretation of the Arab-Israeli conflict

After the First World War, several nation-states emerged from the womb of the Ottoman Empire. Like infants, they metaphorically reflected the dynamics of the separation-individuation stage of development (Mahler, 1958).

Their histories, in my view, were marked by narcissistic disturbances and separation-individuation struggle to define ego boundaries. In Palestine, there were conflicting desires for autonomy over the same territory. The Arabs envisioned an independent Arab Palestine within a federated Syrian state, whereas the Jews had already anticipated the State of Israel.

Thus, the Israeli-Palestinian discord could speak to problematic dynamics of separation and individuation. The Jewish people had already expressed their desire for separation and individuation through the Zionist liberation ideology. However, influenced by their earlier generational traumas, their desire could only be envisioned through an ideological position that denied the other. Individuation and coexistence became irreconcilable; the former could only be achieved at the expense of the latter, and this led them to compulsively repeat their history in their conflict with the Palestinians.

After the dissolution of the Ottoman Empire, Arab Palestinians may have felt abandoned by their dead mother, traumatised and threatened with annihilation. Thus, in a defensive reaction, they sought, on the one hand, to avoid separation and regain their original symbiotic state through unification with Syria, the surrogate mother or parentified sister, and, on the other hand, to focus on Zionist ideology rather than on the underlying desire for individuation of the Jewish people, which they subsequently rejected and interpreted as a murderous Zionist phantasy aimed at exterminating them, the indigenous people of Palestine (Jarrar, 2010). Consequently, they refused to acknowledge the Jewish people's right to independence and the fact that the 1947 UN Partition Plan for Palestine recognised the rights of both the Jewish and Palestinian people to have their respective independent nation-states; they considered it a pro-Zionist proposal because it allocated 62% of the territory to the Jewish state, even though the Palestinian Arab population was twice the size of the Jewish population (Ben-Dror, 2007). Thus, like the Jewish people, Arab Palestinians could not imagine a harmonious coexistence between two autonomous nation-states.

In psychoanalytic terms, the Israeli-Palestinian discord expresses *incestual* (Racamier, 1995) dynamics. *Incestual* refers to a pregenital and narcissistic mode of functioning that has incestuous features but not necessarily incestuous enactments. The *incestual* aims to avoid intrapsychic conflicts and *primal mourning* (Racamier, 1992); the latter is a psychic work of separation by which the ego mourns its symbiosis with the mother and renounces total possession of the object, thus restructuring its object relations and achieving differentiation. Hence, the Israelis and Palestinians, apparently failing to do the necessary work of *primal mourning* (Racamier, 1992), were locked into perennial mourning. Their desire to individuate and become independent nation-states triggered feelings of guilt, earlier traumas and loss. To protect themselves, they transmuted the beliefs that founded their groups, organised their lives and created their sense of collective identity, belonging and common purpose (Kaës, 2016; Kernberg, 2003) into an *incestual*, alienating, defensive and paranoid *closing ideology* (Kaës, 2016)—an ideology of entitlement (Volkan, 2009). They shored their identities on the identity of the group, replacing their ideals with those of the group. As a result, Israelis and Palestinians became subservient to the ideas, ideals and idols of their ideology (Kaës, 2016).

Idolatry originates from the fourth group basic assumption, *Incohesion: aggregation/massification or (ba) I: A/M*, whereby the group function as either an individualistic aggregate or a fusional and confusional mass (Hopper, 2009; Hopper & Weinberg, 2018). To Hopper (2009), *massification* expresses a *hysterical idealisation* of the group as a whole as well as the leader and identification with them and the individual group members, which generate 'feelings of pseudo-morale and illusions of well-being' (p. 225). The *massification* pole of group incohesion expresses the desire to merge with the maternal hallucinated mind and body. The large group becomes an idealised mother—the *good breast*—who heals their narcissistic injuries (Chasseguet-Smirgel, 1985).

The Israelis and Palestinians entertained the phantasy of an idealised sect, replacing the collapse of their phantasies of returning to the mother's womb, the primitive scene or the cannibalistic murder of the father with undemocratic phantasies that perpetuate violence (Duparc, 2004). They fused with each other and with their leader, their land and their ideals (Chasseguet-Smirgel, as cited in Ostow, 1996), their ideologies of entitlement marked by the dream of recovering all the lost lands currently occupied by others (Volkan, 2007). The talionic law replaced the social law—forbidding without protecting; Thanatos, omnipotence, enactment and repetition compulsion directed their group dynamics. Internal objects failed to structure their psychic lives. Archaic violence became rampant, and fear overwhelmed their relationships (Freud, 1921).

Israeli and Palestinian societies are locked in a deadly conflict over the same land, their separation and individuation from the womb of the Ottoman Empire reactivating their *primary narcissism* (Freud, 1914), which denotes an objectless stage of undifferentiation, preceding the recognition of the object, as well as their archaic anxieties, and earlier traumas. These fears of annihilation are linked to intrauterine and birth experiences (Hopper & Weinberg, 2018). Against fragmentation and annihilation fears, both groups seem to have remained or regressed into a state of incohesion (Hopper, 2009; Hopper & Weinberg, 2018). Borders are a shared symbolic skin that protects group identity (Volkan, 2004). Therefore, drawing and maintaining borders took on life and death connotations for the respective groups, with each claiming land ownership and denying the legitimacy of the other. The process of separation and individuation for Israelis and Palestinians, ostensibly having difficulty with primordial mourning, mutated into violent clashes, compulsively repeating earlier traumatic experiences and unconsciously passing them on from generation to generation.

The dissolution of the Ottoman Empire may have revived the earlier traumas of persecution and expulsion, as well as the annihilation anxieties of the Jewish people living there. The Ottoman Empire had become a containing and protective womb for the persecuted Jews of Western and Central Europe, as well as for the Sephardic Jews who, fleeing the Spanish Inquisition, immigrated to Turkey, among other countries, joining the Jewish communities already there (Stora & Meddeb, 2013). In addition, Hitler's rise to power in the early 1920s and his Nazi genocidal ideology exacerbated their earlier traumas. As a result, Jews living in the Empire may have felt an urgent need to preserve a protective and containing motherland. The Zionist liberation movement, founded by European Jews as a project of individuation for all Jews, took off, but at the expense of the other inhabitants of the region.

Israelis and Palestinians behaved like a horde of brothers. The *fraternal complex* (Kaës, 2008), an unconscious intrapsychic triangular organisation (ego-mother/father-sibling) which regulates relationships on a horizontal level, as opposed to the Oedipal complex which regulates relationships on a vertical axis (ego-mother-father), mutated into an archaic form with the imago of the primal mother and feelings of hatred, envy and jealousy prevailing. The sibling trauma (Mitchell, 2006, 2013a, 2013b, 2014) was reactivated. The primal fratricidal phantasy of Cain against Abel (Qabil against Habil), enacted in the Bible and the Koran, was re-enacted. The mutual hatred and violence between Israelis and Palestinians may reveal the conflicting desires to possess the same part of the former Ottoman territory. It expresses an unconscious archaic desire to expel the intrusive rival brother and become the mother's phallus and the exclusive owner of her womb (Kaës, 2008). Paradoxically, although the siblings cannot live together, it is fatal for them to separate and individuate (Caillot & Decherf, 1982).

The Israeli-Palestinian conflict became one of life and death, of self-preservation and phallic narcissistic affirmation juxtaposed with the desire to destroy the other, perceived as a part object (Kaës, 2008). The rule became 'expel or be expelled; kill or be killed'. Group members also entertained the unconscious desire for collective death (Ruffiot, 1985), which underlines the impossibility of recreating good symbiotic experiences other than through collective death to restore peace. These collective death phantasies—and the defence against these phantasies through the sacrifice, murder or suicide of a group member—express the warring groups' difficulty in symbolising loss and trauma. The two regressed groups reverted to split thinking and prejudice. Thus, according to Brenner (2009), all Palestinians became Muslim terrorists and all Israeli Jews became persecuting Nazis plotting to control the world.

To cope with the helplessness that trauma produces and to preserve their threatened internal objects, Israelis and Palestinians alike, in a state of pathological narcissism operating under the aegis of the death drive, denied their kinship and interdependence, preserving infantile omnipotence (Racamier, 1989). Palestinians defended themselves against annihilation and abandonment anxieties through the *amoeboid* massification pole of group in-cohesion (Hopper, 2009). They sought to merge with other Arab countries to realise the dream of an Arab Kingdom of Syria.

Meanwhile, existing Jewish communities and immigrants fleeing Hitler, traumatised by centuries of persecution, defended themselves against the fear of engulfment through the crustacean and schizoid aggregation pole of group incohesion (Hopper, 2009). The Jewish people developed a group *self-engendering phantasy* (Racamier, 1989, 1992, 1995). Through this phantasy, the individual has the illusion of being born of oneself without parents, being one's own parent or being the parent of one's parents. When attachments to internal objects are seen as vampiric, the individual uses this phantasy to stop the narcissistic depletion that threatens to overwhelm their fragile ego bound-aries. As with the *self-engendering phantasy*, the basic assumption *I:A/M*, which is an acronym for *Incohesion: Aggregation/Massification*, is also an 'I am'. In other words, it is an affirmation when identity is threatened (Hopper, 2009). Thus, the Jewish people may not have been inclined to forge frater-nal ties with the Arab communities of British-mandated Palestine. Moreover, with the ego boundaries of their newly established nation-state still fragile, they feared that their Arab neighbours would vampirise and devour them. As a result, the Jewish people found themselves completely cut off from and at war with their Arab neighbours, unconsciously self-fulfilling their prophecy of annihilation and engulfment.

Thus, Israelis and Palestinians could not forge fraternal bonds under the aegis of the symbolic and *Oedipal fraternal complex*, characterised by the interplay of hatred, envy and jealousy, on the one hand, and love, ambiva-lence and identification with the other sibling, on the other (Kaës, 2008). Both denied the 'good' elements of their histories and attacked their links (Bion, 1959) and the operation of linking itself via unbinding, or decathexis. In do-ing so, they actualised the *disobjectalising* function of Thanatos, which at-tacks the object, the *objectalising* or investing process and, in extreme cases, the ego itself (Green 2012). They forgot the 14 centuries of cohabitation in which Jews, Christians and Arabs lived together in cooperation and 'religious symbiosis', creating a specific culture and civilisation (Ostow, 1996; Stora & Meddeb, 2013). For example, during the Middle Ages, Jews freely and regu-larly interacted with their Muslim siblings, collaborating with them, lending them money and vice versa (Stora & Meddeb, 2013). They also occupied a permanent position within the Islamic social structure and, although margin-alised by their dhimmi status, were not excluded or exiled.

During Ottoman rule, the discriminated communities perceived Muslim governance positively. Jews, in particular, were perceived as accomplices of the Ottomans. Their capital, knowledge and diverse skills were beneficial and indispensable to the development and prosperity of the Empire. Jewish doc-tors and businessmen also exerted diplomatic influence, albeit semi-officially (Stora & Meddeb, 2013).

Moreover, Israelis and Palestinians forgot the link that unites their traditions: their two religions 'are not only religions of the Book, but also of the Law' (Stora & Meddeb, 2013, p. 24); they debate identical central issues from analogous moral and ethical perspectives and share the same religious characters and stories, despite their differences in interpretation. The Arabs forgot that Islamic culture, from conception to medieval Spain and the Ottoman Empire, had tended towards tolerance and harmony among the Children of Abraham or the People of the Book—Jews, Muslims and Christians (Ramzy, 2007). They selectively recalled the turbulent relations between the Prophet and the existing Jewish tribes, characterised by political rivalry despite religious proximity (Stora & Meddeb, 2013).

Islam has attempted to converge with Judaism before later differentiating itself from it (Stora & Meddeb, 2013). When the Prophet went to Medina, he claimed that he was the prophet the Jews were waiting for, and when they refused to acknowledge him as such, he became disappointed and frustrated (Stora & Meddeb, 2013). He also discovered that the Prophet Ishmael was the son of Abraham and the forefather of the Arabs, who worshipped God like Abraham, Isaac and Jacob (Ishmael, 2023). The Prophet thus identified himself and Islam as the legitimate descendants of Abraham. This connection to Ishmael and Abraham provided a theological foundation for Islam. It facilitated an Islamic assertiveness that led to violent confrontations with the Jewish community, driven by both political and religious motives, including the desire to challenge the hegemony of the Jewish tribes and the revelation to the Prophet of hostile Koranic verses that portrayed the 'disobedient children of Israel as incurring God's wrath' (Stora & Meddeb, 2013, p. 16).

When the Israeli-Palestinian conflict erupted, it reactivated earlier traumas for both parties. Arabs recalled the political hegemony of the Jewish tribes in the western Arabian Peninsula and the persecution of the Prophet in his hometown of Quraish, which led him to flee to Medina, where he was shamefully snubbed as the expected prophet of the Jews. They also recalled the subsequent sacrilegious wars between the Prophet and these tribes, and probably the Muslim defeat at the Battle of Uhud. Jews recalled their expulsion from the Arabian Peninsula and the shame of being subjected to the discriminatory, inferior, second-class, albeit protected, civil status of the Islamic dhimmi system, which was interpreted as 'universal anti-Semitism' (Stora & Meddeb, 2013, p. 592). Israel's economic, political and military superiority and hegemony, in a compulsive repetition, apparently reversed the dhimmi system. It created an asymmetry in which the Palestinians found themselves relegated to second-class citizenship. The siblings of the *archaic fraternal complex* (Kaës, 2008) can never be similar or equal.

Additionally, the Israeli-Palestinian conflict seems to have reactivated the pathological triangle between Abraham, Sarah and Hagar for the two warring groups, as well as the sibling rivalry between the two half-brothers, Ishmael and Isaac, and between them and their father, Abraham. According to the King James Bible (1769/2023; Genesis 16, 17), the barren Sarah offered her Egyptian maid Hagar to her husband Abraham to have a son and fulfil the Abrahamic covenant. When Hagar began to disrespect Sarah, she was treated harshly, prompting her to flee into the desert. There Hagar met God's Angel, who told her that she would bear a son, Ishmael, from whom God would make a great nation, as God later confirmed to Abraham. When Ishmael was 13 years old, God told Abraham that his wife Sarah would give birth to a son named Isaac, with whom he would establish His covenant. Thus, according to the King James Bible (1769/2023; Genesis, 17), Isaac was the true heir of the Abrahamic tradition and covenant, while Ishmael was blessed with a great nation. After the birth of Isaac, and at Sarah's insistence, Abraham banished Hagar and her son Ishmael to the desert.

In banishing Ishmael to the desert and forging his covenant with Isaac, Abraham pitted his two sons against each other. His act lies at the root of the primordial sibling conflict that the Jews and Muslims are still enacting (Roith, 2006). However, the Holy Father, not Abraham, chose to forge the covenant with the son. This choice might be at the roots of the shame and victimhood with which Arabs and Palestinians struggle. The Holy Father seems to compulsively pit one son against the other, triggering the *archaic fraternal complex*. He had already chosen to accept Abel's sacrifice and reject Cain's (Genesis 4:1–5), which pitted the first two sons of Adam and Eve after their expulsion from the Garden of Eden against each other. When Cain, the first-born, killed his younger brother, Abel, out of jealousy, God banished him from His presence, making him a restless wanderer of the earth. The exodus saga is repeated compulsively. One son is repetitively expelled, becoming a homeless wanderer.

Additionally, God commanded Abraham to take his beloved son to Mount Moriah to sacrifice him as a burnt offering (Genesis 22:2–18). However, when Abraham was about to slay his son at the sacrificial altar, God's Angel stopped him and directed him to sacrifice a nearby ram as a substitute. Judaism and Islam recount the same narrative. However, they differ as to which son should be sacrificed. In Judaism, the son is Isaac, while in Islam, the son's identity is unrevealed and could have been Ishmael. In other words, the Islamic interpretation extends God's covenant beyond the Jews to include Muslims and Arabs.

Essentially, Abraham's family saga speaks, psychoanalytically, of *incestual* family relationships (Racamier, 1995), and an idealised, narcissistic and omnipotent primal father who has access to all women and is willing to sacrifice his sons (Freud, 1939). Indeed, one variant of the infanticidal phantasy is the *incestual* phantasy of returning to the maternal womb, coupled with fratricidal phantasies. Thus, traumatised Israelis and Palestinians re-enacted the *archaic fraternal complex*. The Arab-Israeli conflict can be interpreted as a struggle between different communities over the Holy Land, where Abraham's wife, Sarah, is buried, and Isaac and Ishmael eventually buried their father. (Brenner, 2009). Both Arabs and Jews aspire to retrieve their lost paradise, and both fight over the Holy City of Jerusalem, which the Old Testament compares to a beautiful woman whose breasts of consolation may be suckled (Isaiah, lxvi, 10–11, as cited in Falk, 1974). The lost paradise of intrauterine life would be retrieved, and mourning avoided.

On the one hand, traumatised by centuries of persecution, Jews longed to return to their Promised Land (Brenner, 2009). However, the idea of the Holy Land emerged after the rivalry of European states to partition the Ottoman Empire, making Palestine 'a chosen land, and no longer only promised to a chosen people' (Stora & Meddeb, 2013, p. 293). The Hebrew word for holiness, Kedusha, means separation. Therefore, the idea of the Holy Land can be interpreted to express the Jewish desire to separate and individuate. However, given the traumatic history and complicated mourning of the Jewish people, this desire reactivated the *archaic fraternal complex*. In 1897, Herzl, the founder of the Zionist movement, shared his vision of an exclusive national home for the Jews in 'a country without people for people without a country' (Jarrar, 2010, p. 199). The 1948 *Al-Nakba* or *the Catastrophe*, as Palestinians refer to their expulsion from their motherland, can be interpreted as an enactment of the desire to expel the rival sibling and take sole possession of the maternal womb; the State of Israel denied the physical, national, social and cultural existence of the indigenous Palestinian people, and their desires, anxieties and conflicts.

On the other hand, the expelled and traumatised Palestinians see themselves as 'a nation in quest of a homeland' (Stora & Meddeb, 2013, p. 395). They also see Palestine as a lost paradise and an idealised mother who fails to heal their injuries (Jarrar, 2010). Their expulsion from their motherland in 1948 gave rise to a national ideology and movement in exile dedicated to 'al-Awda, the battle for the return to Palestine' (Stora & Meddeb, 2013, p. 383). Believing their separation from their homeland to be temporary, Palestinians avoided the psychic pain linked to mourning. Separation and object loss would not, given their temporary character, entail the loss of an ego part.

Final reflections

Israelis and Palestinians, in their processes of separation and individuation from the womb of the mother Ottoman Empire, seem to be re-enacting the biblical Exodus trauma. The biblical Exodus of the Israelites from Egypt is a founding myth or state ideology for the Jewish people, and the Palestinian exodus can be interpreted as an inverse-compulsive repetition. It is as if, with time collapse and transmission of shared trauma, Israelis have identified with the Egyptian oppressor (Volkan, 2004, 2013). In addition, Palestinians have identified with the victimised and expelled Jews. History has repeated itself, with the logic of 'expel or be expelled.'

However, the biblical Exodus refers not only to the victimisation of the Israelites but also to their liberation from Egyptian bondage and their covenant with God (Bandstra, 2008), who will always protect them as *His chosen people* on the condition that they respect His laws and worship only Him. In psychoanalytic terms, this covenant is an unconscious alliance (Kaës, 2014) sealed among human beings to identify with the symbolic father and renounce the direct realisation of destructive drives. However, this fraternal pact has apparently failed to move the people of the Middle East from a talionic state of primitive horde mentality to a state of law mentality that prohibits incest, cannibalism and murder. Israeli and Palestinian group *incestual* functioning continues to structure individual psychic lives of its members and their intersubjective links. The Israeli ideology of return to the Holy Land and the Palestinian doctrine of the *Right of Return* express the desire to return to the womb. The process of separation and individuation remains complicated for both groups. It is the primacy of pregenital functioning and the difficulty of *primal mourning*. Access to the covenant of reason (the reality principle and secondary process thinking) remains barred.

Palestinian extreme parties refuse to recognise Israel's legitimacy, while both Israel and the West, in their pact, deny their guilt—the West for persecuting the Jews and the Israelis for persecuting the Palestinians (Kemp, 2011). This Jewish-Western pact created a perverse triangulation. Western states compulsively repeated the *bystander position* (Cohen, as cited in Kemp, 2011) they had taken towards fascism two generations ago. It is as if the Western father Abraham had once again chosen one wife over the other and one son over the other. Sarah, the legitimate wife/motherland, became Israel, whereas Hagar, the maid/motherland, became Palestine. The Jews became the chosen Isaac, whereas the Palestinians became the expelled and rowdy Ishmael. Shared shame, humiliation and guilt are transmitted through repeated trauma. The primacy of the *incestual* and pregenital continues. Only one womb can be recognised and returned to either Sarah's or Hagar's. The other, in an envious attack, must be obliterated. Similar to the two mothers, Sarah and Hagar, the two motherlands, Israel and Palestine, cannot co-exist for the time being. The Israelis must avenge their mother for Hagar's disdain, whereas the Palestinians must avenge Hagar for her expulsion into the desert—an expulsion that may represent the *primal exodus*. Additionally, Israelis and Palestinians, in identification with the primal father Abraham, enact the infanticide phantasy by transforming it into fratricidal massacres; each kills the other, identified as the sacrificial son.

References

Bandstra, B. L. (2008). *Reading the Old Testament: an introduction to the Hebrew bible*. New York: Wadsworth: Cengage Learning.
Beker, A. (2005). The forgotten narrative: Jewish refugees from Arab countries. *Jewish Political Studies Review, 17*: 3–4.

Ben-Dror, E. (2007). The Arab struggle against partition: The international arena of summer 1947. *Middle Eastern Studies*, *43*(2): 259–293. https://doi.org/10.1080/00263200601114117.

Biger, G. (1981). Where was Palestine? Pre-World War I perception. *Area*, *13*(2): 153–160.

Biger, G. (2008). The boundaries of Israel—Palestine past, present, and future: A critical geographical view. *Israel Studies*, *13*(1): 68–93.

Bion, W. R. (1959). Attacks on linking. *International Journal of Psycho-Analysis, 40*: 308–315. https://doi.org/10.1002/j.2167-4086.2013.00029.x

Brenner, I. (2009). The Palestinian/Israeli conflict: A geopolitical identity disorder. *American Journal of Psychoanalysis*, *69*(1): 62–71. https://doi.org/10.1057/ajp.2008.42

Caillot, J. P., & Decherf, G. (1982). *Thérapie Familiale Psychanalytique et Paradoxalité* [*Psychoanalytic family therapy and paradoxicality*]. Paris: Clancier-Guénaud.

Chasseguet-Smirgel, J. (1985). The ego ideal and the psychology of groups. *Free Associations 1, 2*: 31–60.

Duparc, F. (2004). *Le mal des idéologies [The evil of ideologies]*. Paris: PUF.

Falk, A. (1974). Border symbolism. *Psychoanalytic Quarterly*, *43*(4): 650–660. https://doi.org/10.1080/21674086.1974.11926691

Freud, S. (1914). On narcissism. In: J. Strachey (Ed.), *The standard edition of the complete psychological works of Sigmund Freud, Volume XIV (1914–1916): On the history of the psycho-analytic movement, papers on metapsychology and other works* (pp. 67–102). London: The Hogarth Press.

Freud, S. (1921). Group psychology and the analysis of the ego. In: J. Strachey (Ed.), *The standard edition of the complete psychological works of Sigmund Freud, Volume XVIII (1920–1922): Beyond the pleasure principle* (pp. 65–144). London: The Hogarth Press.

Freud, S. (1939). Moses and monotheism: Three essays. In: J. Strachey (Ed.), *The standard edition of the complete psychological works of Sigmund Freud, Volume XXIII* (pp. 1–138). London: The Hogarth Press.

Gerber, H. (1998). 'Palestine' and other territorial concepts in the 17th century. *International Journal of Middle East Studies*, *30*(4): 563–572. https://doi.org/10.1017/s0020743800052569

Green, A. (2012). *Key ideas for a contemporary psychoanalysis: Misrecognition and recognition of the unconscious*. London & New York: Routledge.

Hopper, E. (2009). The theory of the basic assumption of incohesion: Aggregation/massification or (BA) I: A/M. *British Journal of Psychotherapy*, *25*: 214–229.

Hopper, E., & Weinberg, H. (2018). *The social unconscious in persons, groups and societies: Mainly theory*. The new international library of group analysis book (Kindle edition, Vol. 1). London & New York: Routledge.

Ishmael. (2023, January 16). *Encyclopedia*. Retrieved from https://www.encyclopedia.com/people/philosophy-and-religion/biblical-proper-names-biographies/ishmael

Jarrar, A. (2010). Palestinian suffering: Some personal, historical, and psychoanalytic reflections. *International Journal of Applied Psychoanalytic Studies*, *7*(3): 197–208. https://doi.org/10.1002/aps.252

Kaës, R. (2008). *Le Complexe Fraternel [The fraternal complex]*. Paris: Dunod.

Kaës, R. (2014). *Les alliances inconscientes* [Unconscious alliances]. Paris: Dunod. https://doi.org/10.3917/dunod.kaes.2014.01.

Kaës, R. (2016). *L'idéologie, l'idéal, l'idée, l'idole [The ideology, the ideal, the idea, the idol]*. Paris: Dunod. https://doi.org/10.3917/dunod.kaese.2016.01

Kark, R. (1994). *American consuls in the Holy Land, 1832–1914*. Detroit: Wayne State University Press.

Kemp, M. (2011). Dehumanization, guilt and large group dynamics with reference to the West, Israel and the Palestinians. *British Journal of Psychotherapy, 27*(4): 383–405. https://doi.org/10.1111/j.1752-0118.2011.01250.x.

Kernberg, O. F. (2003). Sanctioned social violence: A psychoanalytic view-Part I. *International Journal of Psycho-Analysis, 84*(3): 683–698. https://doi.org/10.1516/002075703766644913

King James Bible. (2023). *King James Bible* (Kindle edition). Green World Classics. (Original work published 1769).

Lewis, B. (1980). Palestine: On the history and geography of a name. *The International History Review, 2*(1): 1–12. https://doi.org/10.1080/07075332.1980.9640202

Mahler, M. S. (1958). Autism and symbiosis, two extreme disturbances of identity. *International Journal of Psycho-Analysis, 39*: 77–82.

Mitchell, J. (2006). From infant to child: The sibling trauma, the rite de passage, and the construction of the "Other" in the social group. *Fort Da, 12*: 35–49.

Mitchell, J. (2013a). Siblings: Thinking theory. *Psychoanalytic Study of the Child, 67*: 14–34.

Mitchell, J. (2013b). The law of the mother: Sibling trauma and the brotherhood of war. *Canadian Journal of Psychoanalysis, 21*:145–159.

Mitchell, J. (2014). Siblings and the psychosocial. *Organizational and Social Dynamics, 14*: 1–12.

Ostow, M. (1996). Myth and madness: A report of a psychoanalytic study of antisemitism. *International Journal of Psycho-Analysis, 77*(1): 15–31.

Ostow, M. (2007). Commentary on 'Mass hatred in the Muslim and Arab world: The neglected problem of anti-semitism' by Neil Kresse. *International Journal of Applied Psychoanalytic Studies, 4*: 221–234.

Porath, Y. (1974). *The emergence of the Palestinian–Arab national movement, 1918–1929*. London: Frank Cass.

Racamier, P. C. (1989). *Antœdipe et ses Destins [Antoedipus and its destinies]*. Paris: Apsygée.

Racamier, P. C. (1992). *Le Génie des Origines [The genius of origins]*. Paris: Payot and Rivage.

Racamier, P. C. (1995). *L'inceste et l'incestuel [The incest and the incestual]* Paris: Éditions du Collège.

Ramzy, N. (2007). Commentary on 'Mass hatred in the Muslim and Arab world: The neglected problem of anti-semitism' by Neil Kressel. *International Journal of Applied Psychoanalytic Studies, 4*(3): 191–196. https://doi.org/10.1002/aps.152

Ramzy, N., Awad, G. A., Strenger, C., & Portuges, S. (2007). The application of psychoanalytic thinking to social problems: analytic perspectives on the Palestinian–Israeli conflict. *International Journal of Applied Psychoanalytic Studies, 4*(3): 286–294. https://doi.org/10.1002/aps.146

Roith, E. (2006). Ishmael and Isaac: An enduring conflict. In: P. Coles (Ed.), *Sibling relationships* (pp. 49–74). London: Karnac.

Ruffiot, A. (1985). Originaire et imaginaire: Le souhait de mort collective en thérapie familiale psychanalytique [Original and imaginary: The collective death wish in psychoanalytic family therapy]. *Gruppo, Revue de Psychanalyse Groupale, 1*: 69–85.

Stora, B., & Meddeb, A. (2013). *A history of Jewish–Muslim relations: From the origins to the present day*. Princeton, NJ: Princeton University Press.

The Book of Genesis. (2023). Retrieved from https://mechon-mamre.org/p/pt/pt0116. htm, https://mechon-mamre.org/p/pt/pt0117.htm, and https://mechon-mamre.org/p/ pt/pt0122.htm (Chapters 16, 17, and 22).

Volkan, V. D. (2004). *Blind trust: Large groups and their leaders in times of crisis and terror.* Charlottesville, VA: Pitchstone Publishing.

Volkan, V. D. (2007). Not letting go: From individual perennial mourners to societies with entitlement ideologies. In: F. Glocer Fiorini, S. Lewkowicz, & T. Bokanowski (Eds.), *On Freud's mourning and melancholia* (pp. 90–109). London: International Psychoanalytic Association.

Volkan, V. D. (2009). The next chapter: consequences of societal trauma. In: P. Gobodo-Madikizela & C. Van Der Merwe (Eds.), *Memory, narrative and forgiveness: Perspectives of the unfinished journeys of the past* (pp. 1–26). Cambridge: Cambridge Scholars Publishing.

Volkan, V. (2013). Large-group-psychology in its own right: large-group identity and peace-making. *International Journal of Applied Psychoanalytic Studies*, *10*(3): 210–246. https://doi.org/10.1002/aps.1368.

Chapter 5

Hamas
The ideology of brotherhood

On 7 October 2023, the Gaza-based Palestinian Sunni Islamist organisation Hamas, in conjunction with several other Palestinian militant groups, orchestrated terrorist attacks to mark the 50th anniversary of the 1973 Yom Kippur War between Syria, Egypt and Israel (Meyer, 2024). It was the first time since the 1948 Arab-Israeli war that Israeli territory had been infiltrated. Palestinian armed groups, including Hamas, called the attacks Operation Al-Aqsa Flood or 'Tufan Al-Aqsa' in Arabic (United Nations, 2023). It resulted in the deaths of mostly innocent civilians and the capture of hostages who were taken to Gaza.

According to Hamas, the attack was a response to the ongoing Israeli occupation of the Palestinian territories, the blockade of Gaza, the growth of illegal Israeli settlements, increased violence by Israeli settlers and recent escalations (McKernan et al., 2023). The raid was condemned by many countries as an act of terrorism, while some Arab and Muslim nations blamed Israel's occupation of Palestinian territories for the attack. The raid was seen as Israel's most significant military setback since the 1973 Arab-Israeli war and has been described as the deadliest in Israel's history and the worst for Jews since the Holocaust. Some have even described it as a genocidal massacre of Israelis (McKernan et al., 2023).

The initial raid marked the beginning of the ongoing war between Israel and Hamas. In retaliation for the Hamas attack, Israel declared a state of war for the first time since the 1973 Yom Kippur War. The Israel Defence Forces (IDF) launched air strikes on Gaza for the first time since the Second Intifada, a popular uprising against Israeli rule that lasted from 2000 to 2005. A few weeks later, ground troops and armoured vehicles entered the Gaza Strip. By 2024, thousands of Palestinians in Gaza had lost their lives and many more have been forced to flee, while more than half of Gaza's structures were either destroyed or damaged (The Editors of Encyclopaedia Britannica, 2024).

While the conflict has been concentrated in Gaza, it has spread beyond that region. The IDF entered Rafah and intensified its attacks in the West Bank, imposing blockades on many areas. In October, Israeli settlers intensified their attacks on Palestinians. Conflicts with Hezbollah near the Lebanese border

DOI: 10.4324/9781003545842-7

intensified, increasing the risk of a second front opening. Houthi forces also attacked southern Israel with rockets and drones, suggesting possible coordination between members of the Iran-led 'axis of resistance'. In April 2024, Israeli warplanes targeted the Iranian embassy in Damascus, killing senior members of the Quds Force of the Islamic Revolutionary Guard Corps. In retaliation, Iran launched drones and rockets at Israel, most of which were successfully intercepted. In retaliation, Israel carried out an air strike near a military site in Isfahan, Iran, where activities related to its nuclear programme are carried out. Iran downplayed the situation, saying it was able to intercept the attack (The Editors of Encyclopaedia Britannica, 2024).

The 7 October attack by Hamas and Israel's subsequent violent response to both Hamas and the people of Gaza have provoked a range of conflicting emotions and thoughts in both Israeli and Palestinian communities. Many Israelis advocate severe retaliation, including the deportation of Gazans to Egypt and the destruction of their homes. On the other hand, while some Palestinians privately criticise Hamas for harming innocent civilians and holding women and children hostage, others express pride in Hamas's ability to expose and exploit Israel's vulnerabilities, pointing out that no Palestinian group or Arab nation has been able to do so since 1948 (Klein, 2024). As for Western government, officials have attributed Hamas's attack to its fundamentalist Islamic ideology, which they say has been influenced by the Islamic State of Iraq and Syria (ISIS).

Prior to the 7 October attack, and since its founding in 1987, Hamas has been an important participant in the ongoing Israeli-Palestinian conflict. It has been accused of carrying out suicide bombings and indiscriminate rocket attacks against both Israeli civilians and soldiers, leading to allegations of war crimes by various human rights groups. Several countries have also listed Hamas as a terrorist organisation. However, despite an attempt to condemn Hamas at the United Nations in 2018, the motion was ultimately defeated (United Nations News, 2018).

To analyse the role of Hamas in the intractable Israeli-Palestinian conflict, I will present a group and family psychoanalytic framework, followed by a brief historical overview and a psychoanalytic interpretation of the roots of this political organisation, which originated during the British Mandate of Palestine. By interpreting Hamas's ideological position and behaviour, I hope to provide insight into the unconscious dynamics of the Israeli-Palestinian conflict and contribute to its transformation.

A group and family psychoanalytic framework

I have argued in Chapters 2 and 4 that after the end of the First World War, several nation-states emerged from the womb of the Ottoman Empire. Lebanon, Syria and the British-mandated Palestine struggled and continue to struggle with the challenges of forming distinct and independent nation-states with defined borders. I have also argued that their histories are marked by pregenital *incestual* dynamics (Racamier, 1995) and the difficulty of doing the work of *primal mourning* (Racamier, 1992).

Primal mourning is a universal primal psychic process, by which the ego mourns its symbiosis with the mother and relinquishes total possession of the object. When *primal mourning is avoided,* functioning becomes dominated by *incestuality* (Racamier, 1995), which is a pregenital functioning that fights the desire to separate and individuate and maintains a confusion of boundaries between the Me and the not-Me. *Incestuality* has features of incest but without necessarily incestuous enactment. It is ruled by the death drive and repetition compulsion. Primary process thinking and enactment characterise the functioning of groups and their constituent members.

Thus, I have argued that the struggle of these nation-states stems from their difficulty in mourning their symbiotic relationship. Their blurred geographical boundaries, that is, their body envelopes, have resulted in perforated *psychic envelopes*, or *skin-egos*, which have hindered their ability to adequately distinguish the Me from the not-Me. As a result, their self has remained fragmented. The maternal function of containment and the symbolic paternal function of establishing a post-Oedipal law that both forbids and protects were insufficient.

The newly created nation-states could not contain and symbolise their collective and individual primitive transgenerational anxieties and traumas. The psychic bonds between them and their citizens broke down and violent conflicts erupted between them. The histories of these newly created nation-states were marked by enactments that reflected their need to define their borders and construct solid identities. As a result, they developed *closing ideologies* (Kaës, 2016), which provided an ideological response to misery and shame and were characterised by a paranoid vision of the world that excluded others and otherness. *Closing ideologies* are an attempt at narcissistic reorganisation and a prosthesis for narcissistic fragility, refilling the narcissistic haemorrhage of its perforated container (Benghozi, 2016). These ideologies further complicated the individuation process of the newly created nation-states.

In addition, I have argued in Chapters 2 and 4 that the Lebanese civil wars that lasted from 1975 to 1990 and the Israeli-Palestinian ongoing conflict over land are both enactments of the *archaic fraternal complex* (Kaës, 2008). This complex involves each sibling unconsciously entertaining the phantasy of returning to the mother's womb and aspiring to be her phallus and exclusive owner of her space. In the Lebanese civil wars and the Israeli-Palestinian conflict, each sibling perceived the other as a part object, and in their wars, they enacted the unconscious fratricidal phantasy of this complex.

I have argued in Chapter 3 that Hezbollah was the identified patient and symptom of the *incestual* dynamics and complicated individuation process of its large family nation-state. Similarly, I argue in this chapter that Hamas, as one of the children of British-mandated Palestine, became, through its ideological position, the identified patient and symptom of the complicated dynamics of separation and individuation of the Palestinian people and their avoidance of the work of *primal mourning*. The ideology of Hamas, like that of Hezbollah, is an unconscious prosthesis that compensates for the perforated body envelope of Palestine and thus its fragile sense of self.

To support my psychoanalytic interpretation of the role of Hamas in Palestinian group dynamics, I will next offer a brief historical overview to provide a context for its rise.

A brief historical overview

For centuries, the link between Palestine and Islam has had deep historical and spiritual significance for Muslims. Within the Islamic faith, Palestine is a holy place, as it is for Christians and Jews. Jerusalem in Palestine is also the third holiest city, for Muslims, after Mecca and Medina. The Dome of the Rock, built on the rock from which the Prophet Mohamed ascended to meet God, is believed to be the same place where the Jews built Solomon's Temple. In addition to its religious significance, Palestine served as a geographical bridge between Africa and Asia. Because of its religious and strategic importance, Palestine has been a centre of conflict and conquest (Hroub, 2010).

In AD 638, Muslims gained control of Palestine and ruled it for four centuries. During this time, people of different religious backgrounds were able to coexist peacefully. Since then, Islam has shaped the sociopolitical, cultural and psychological landscape of the region. Later, however, the Crusaders conquered Jerusalem and forcibly integrated it into Christendom. They subjected the Muslim population to brutal massacres and ruled the city for 70 years. They were eventually defeated by Saladin in AD 1187.

Saladin's victory elevated him to a heroic status in Islamic history and imagination. His triumph symbolised the end of Muslim humiliation and defeat, and evoked feelings of pride and glory among Muslims and Palestinians alike. His legacy is a testament to their resilience and ability to overcome challenges (Hroub, 2010). The defeat of the Crusaders by Saladin seems to have become a chosen glory (Volkan, 2013), a shared mental representation of pride and joy that evokes past triumphs in warfare and notable political or religious achievements and heroes. Many Arabs and Palestinians see the European Crusades as the prototype for the Zionist occupation, which also originated in Europe. Moreover, for many Muslims, Palestine being under the control of non-Muslim and foreign rulers, such as the Crusaders in the past and the Zionists in the present, is seen as a defeat for them (Hroub, 2010).

When the Crusaders were totally defeated in 1291, Palestine returned to Muslim rule for seven centuries, first as part of the Mamluk Sultanate, then as part of the Ottoman Empire from 1516 until the end of the First World War. The Islamic roots of the Ottoman Empire linked Palestine to the Arab and Muslim world (Hroub, 2010). However, after the fall of the Empire, the Sykes-Picot Agreement of 1916 redrew the borders of the Middle East and placed the Arab provinces of the Empire under temporary British or French tutelage until permanent political solutions could be implemented. Under the terms of the agreement, the British Mandate was responsible for governing Palestine.

Meanwhile, in an attempt to win the support of various factions in the Middle East, Britain had entered into conflicting agreements with both Arabs and Jews regarding land ownership (Brenner, 2009). The McMahon-Hussein Agreement of 1915 promised the Arabs independence and granted them land in exchange for their help in overthrowing the Ottoman Empire. However, the Balfour Declaration of 1917, heavily influenced by the emerging Zionist movement, supported a Jewish homeland in Palestine and facilitated Jewish immigration to British-controlled Palestine in the 1930s and 1940s, driven by increasing numbers of refugees fleeing Nazi-controlled Europe.

As Zionist settlers sought to establish a Jewish homeland in Palestine with European support, Palestinians responded by mobilising Muslims worldwide to protect Jerusalem and its holy sites. They resisted British rule in the 1920s and 1930s, combining Islam and nationalism as a unifying force. The Izzedin al-Qassam movement emerged in the 1930s as a proud Palestinian jihadist uprising against British colonial forces and increasingly militarised European Zionist settlers (Hroub, 2010).

In 1947, as the international community increasingly supported Jewish settlement, the United Nations proposed a partition plan for Palestine. The following year, amid civil unrest, Britain withdrew from a turbulent Palestine and soon after Israel declared its independence. The Palestinians rejected the partition plan, claiming that it favoured Zionism by giving more land to the Jewish state, even though their population was twice as large as that of the Jews. They refused to acknowledge that the plan recognised the rights of both Jewish and Palestinian people to sovereign nation-states (Ben-Dror, 2007).

With the creation of the State of Israel in 1948, Jews took control of more than half of Palestine, including Jerusalem and were close to the Al-Aqsa Mosque. The Arabs felt betrayed by the Western powers. This defeat was deeply humiliating and a source of shame for Palestinians, Arabs and Muslims. As a result, Islam emerged as a core ideology, deeply rooted in Muslim society, which served to unite against the occupiers and their control over Palestine (Hroub, 2010).

In the 1950s and 1960s, as nationalist and Marxist ideologies shaped Arab and Palestinian movements that sought to oppose Israel and reclaim Palestine, Islamist movements in Palestine and neighbouring states were marginalised (Hroub, 2010).

In 1964, the Palestine Liberation Organisation (PLO) was founded in Jerusalem to liberate historic Palestine and to promote the Palestinian cause. It was initially controlled by Arab states, especially Egypt. However, the increased representation of Palestinian resistance groups within the organisation and the election of Yasser Arafat, a member of the Fatah party, as Chairman of the PLO Executive Committee in the late 1960s shifted power from the Arab states to the Palestinian factions. The PLO emerged as the main political entity for several Palestinian groups and served as Palestine's representative in international institutions. However, the PLO's dependence on neighbouring Arab states made it vulnerable to external influence and exploitation (Passia, 2014).

In 1967, Israel dealt another narcissistic blow to Palestinians and Arabs when it attacked Egypt, Syria and Jordan, seizing Sinai and Gaza from Egypt, the Golan Heights from Syria and the West Bank, East Jerusalem and Al-Aqsa Mosque from Jordan. After this defeat, nationalist and Marxist ideologies began to wane as Palestinian Islamist movements gained momentum. The success of the Iranian revolution in 1979 and the defeat of the PLO in Lebanon in 1982 fuelled their rise. As a result, the Palestinian Islamists came to prominence, overshadowing their secular rival, the Fatah-led Movement for the Liberation of Palestine. This resurgence marked the renewed importance of Islam in Palestinian political dynamics (Hroub, 2010).

In 1982, after its defeat in Lebanon and subsequent exodus, the PLO's separation from its Palestinian support base shifted power from the diaspora to Palestinians in the Occupied Palestinian Territories (OPT). The 1987 First Intifada, or uprising, was also an important moment in Palestinian politics, as it led to the formation of the Unified National Leadership of the Uprising (UNLU), which brought together different factions in the OPT. Although the UNLU eventually merged with the PLO, its leaders were Palestinians from the OPT who challenged the PLO's dominance as the sole representative of Palestinian concerns. This First Intifada also saw the rise of separate groups such as Hamas and Islamic Jihad, which challenged the authority of the PLO (Passia, 2014).

As international attention and support for the Palestinian cause grew, the PLO accepted a two-state solution in the OPT, which was a major concession for the Palestinian people. The PLO was recognised as 'the sole and legitimate representative of the Palestinian people' at the Arab Summit in 1974 (Passia, 2014, p. 2). The PLO was also granted observer status at the United Nations. However, after the Cold War and Arafat's backing of Saddam Hussein during the Gulf War, support for the PLO waned. As a result, the PLO turned its attention to talks with Israel, which eventually led to the 1993 Oslo Accords (Passia, 2014).

Under the Oslo Accords, the PLO and the newly formed Palestinian Authority (PA) were considered separate entities, with the PA acting as a division of the PLO. The PA was given limited administrative and security powers over certain areas of the West Bank and Gaza Strip for a period of five years, with the ultimate aim of establishing a state for the Palestinian people. The PLO's attention shifted from armed conflict and liberation to achieving democratic recognition, governance and statehood. In addition, the dominance of the Fatah faction in the PLO led to its transformation from a liberation organisation to a political party. Fatah's control of the PA also led to its victory in the first Palestinian elections in 1996. This transfer of authority from the PLO to the PA led to disputes between the 'old guard', who had spent their lives in exile, and the 'young guard', who had emerged during the First Intifada.

The Oslo Accords also drew attention to the overlapping roles and responsibilities of the PLO and the PA, resulting in unclear lines of authority and overlapping membership. The PLO, PA and Fatah were all intertwined, with the success of the Oslo Accords crucial to Fatah's legitimacy and influence within the PA. This made it difficult to distinguish between the PLO and the PA, which hindered good governance and transparency (Passia, 2014).

When the five-year interim process established by the Oslo Accords failed to meet either Israeli or Palestinian expectations, a summit between the United States, Israel and the Palestinians was convened at Camp David in 2000 to resolve the Israeli-Palestinian conflict. Despite the efforts made, the parties were unable to reach an agreement.

Hamas: ideology and the *archaic fraternal complex*

Hamas, both an acronym for Harakat al-Muqawama al-Islamiyyah (Islamic Resistance Movement) and an Arabic word meaning 'zeal', is the Palestinian jihadist organisation founded in 1987 as an extension of the Palestinian branch of the Muslim Brotherhood in Egypt (Jefferis, 2016; Levitt, 2006). For Hamas supporters, both meanings of the acronym and the Arabic word are central to a belief system that advocates Palestinian nationalism within an Islamic framework.

In 1973, Sheikh Ahmad Yassin founded Hamas as a charitable organisation linked to the Muslim Brotherhood called Mujama al-Islamiya.

In 1987, Hamas emerged in the Gaza Strip in response to the First Intifada. In 1988, it published its founding charter, which stated its refusal to recognise the Jewish state of Israel and its intention to eradicate it and establish an Islamic state in its place (Baconi, 2018; Freedman, 2019; Hroub, 2010).

According to Hamas's 1988 charter, all of British-mandated Palestine, stretching from the Mediterranean Sea to the Jordan River, was to be freed from Zionist control and converted into an Islamic Waqf, providing a sense of security and protection for people of different faiths to live together in harmony. The charter emphasised the indivisibility of 'historic Palestine' and referred to it as an Islamic territory entrusted to Muslims until the Day of Judgment (Baconi, 2018).

By emphasising the indivisibility of the land of 'historic Palestine', Hamas ideology expresses the Palestinian avoidance of the work of *primal mourning* (Racamier, 1992). The Palestinian collective seems to deny its castration from the Ottoman Empire. As a result, they identified themselves with their

Muslim brothers from the Arab states who emerged from the womb of the Ottoman Empire. They enacted their complicated dynamics of separation and individuation by embracing an ideology that sought unity with a Muslim community or umma, a metaphorical surrogate mother's womb to replace the loss of British-mandated Palestine.

While Hamas was formally founded on 14 December 1987, its roots can be traced back to 1967, when it emerged as an arm of the Muslim Brotherhood in Palestine. Its history goes back even further than 1967 (Levitt, 2006). Founded in Egypt in 1928 during the decline of the Ottoman Empire, the Muslim Brotherhood was one of the pioneering Islamic movements in the region. It has established branches in almost every Arab country, with the Palestinian branch created in Jerusalem in 1946. The primary goal of each Muslim Brotherhood movement is to establish an Islamic state in its respective country, with the ultimate vision of uniting all Islamic nations into one Muslim community (Hroub, 2010).

Thus, Hamas, as a Palestinian subgroup of the Muslim Brotherhood, appears to be driven by pre-phallic phantasies of confraternity and complementarity (Kancyper, 2011). It sought to create a magical, omnipotent and inseparable brotherhood united by *primary narcissism* (Freud, 1914), which denotes an objectless stage of undifferentiation that precedes the recognition of the object. The Muslim Brotherhood became the containing primal mother to the Palestinian people.

Moreover, in its ideological kinship with the Muslim Brotherhood, Hamas seems to be seeking a sibling relationship that can mediate between siblings in response to the loss of the motherland to the newborn Israel. When the State of Israel declared its independence in 1948, the Palestinian people felt traumatised and struggled with unsymbolised annihilation anxieties. In their trauma of being replaced and displaced, they treated the 'other' as the hated baby, the non-human. The *sibling trauma* (Mitchell, 2014) of the Palestinian people eventually culminated in an ideological position embodied by Hamas.

Hamas's brotherhood ideology expresses the dynamics of the *archaic fraternal complex* (Kaës, 2008) of the Palestinian people, with the unconscious archaic desire to expel the intrusive rival sibling and to become the mother's phallus and the exclusive owner of her womb (Kaës, 2008). It speaks to the conflicting desires of Palestinians to possess the same piece of the former Ottoman territory. To gain exclusive possession of their motherland womb, the Palestinian people perceived their rival sibling as a part object or an appendix of their 'mother' land or their own imaginary body that must be eliminated (Kaës, 2008). Elimination is necessary because the rival sibling threatens their individuality, undermines their omnipotence and hurts their narcissism. Thus, the ongoing conflict between Palestinians and Israelis has developed into a deep-seated animosity that symbolises a struggle between life and death, self-preservation and the desperate need for phallic narcissistic affirmation, juxtaposed with the desire to destroy the other who is perceived as a part object (Kaës, 2008). The rule became 'expel or be expelled; kill or be killed'. According to Mitchell (2006, 2013a, 2013b, 2014), Hamas's brotherhood ideology violates the 'law of the mother', which prohibits murder.

Hamas's main slogan, enshrined in Article 8 of its charter, emphasises the importance of violent jihad, which is seen as a religiously acceptable form of resistance against those perceived as enemies of Islam. Jihad in Arabic means 'struggle' and has two different connotations: the first refers to armed struggle and the use of force, while the second refers to individual efforts to embody moral excellence and adhere to divine guidance. Alternatively, jihad can encompass efforts to fight injustice and oppression, to promote and protect Islam and to create a just community through preaching, education and even holy war. Given its endorsement of suicide bombings and acts of terrorism, Hamas interprets jihad as violent opposition to perceived enemies of Islam (Levitt, 2006).

Hamas thus emerged as a religious nationalist liberation movement with a dual mission of promoting the Islamic faith and advocating armed resistance against Israel. While some saw Hamas as a continuation of the PLO's efforts, others saw it as a necessary addition to the Palestinian national struggle, which was in danger of surrendering to Israel. Unlike the PLO and other Arab nations such as Egypt and Jordan, which had signed peace agreements with Israel, Hamas rejected peaceful approaches and remained steadfast in its goal of liberating Palestine. It refused to align itself with the PLO and instead remained committed to the original goal of liberating Palestine as set out by the PLO founders in the 1960s. Furthermore, it opposed any peace agreement that required full recognition of Israel's right to exist (Hroub, 2010).

Between 1988 and 1995, Hamas faced a number of ideological and political challenges. These included managing the tension between its identity as a Palestinian nationalist movement and its Islamic message, which was intended to appeal to a wider audience. It has also struggled with the conflict between its self-image as a political movement and the strict principles outlined in its charter. Hamas's identity crises can be seen as a mirror reflection and symptom of the Palestinian identity crisis. A further complication for Hamas was its evolving relationship with the PLO. In response, Hamas adopted three strategies for political action: competing with the PLO, working to prevent conflict within the Arab world and establishing formal channels of communication to address core disagreements with the PLO. However, the signing of the PLO-Israeli Accords brought about a significant change in the dynamics of the Hamas-PLO relationship. What had once been a competition between two seemingly equal entities became a relationship between a ruling authority and an opposition group (Klein, 1996).

The *archaic fraternal complex* seems to be the underlying force influencing Palestinians' relations with each other and with their Jewish siblings. This complex undermined their ability to unite in a good enough manner to create a sovereign Palestinian nation-state. They remained in a state of *primary narcissism*, part objects, divided into opposing political subgroups, clinging to *closing ideologies*. According to Volkan (2004), these subgroups provide Palestinians with a sense of narcissistic control and a solid group identity that compensated for the lack of a distinct Palestinian identity. As a result, the Palestinian political parties became embroiled in internal conflicts and *closing ideologies*. These sociopolitical and religious ideologies serve as a collective defence mechanism and unconscious alliance to suppress the traumatic elements associated with catastrophes.

In Chapter 4, I argued that the Zionist ideology, which sought to create a Jewish state in what the Romans called Palestine, was a response to a long history of European persecution and anti-Semitism. Similarly, the ideology of Hamas could be a response to a series of catastrophes, including (1) the disintegration of the Ottoman Empire and the British colonisation of Palestine; (2) the ām al-nakbah (the year of the catastrophe) of 1920, which marked the year of the deposition of King Faysal by the French and shattered the aspirations of a sovereign Arab Palestine within a federated Syrian state; and (3) the al-Nakba (the Catastrophe) of 1948, which followed Israel's declaration of independence and the subsequent Israeli-Palestinian war that resulted in the expulsion of the Palestinians from their homeland.

Both Zionist and Hamas ideologies serve similar visions. Hamas's 1988 charter resembles the Zionist vision of more or less the same territory. Although there are countless variations in defining the exact boundaries of the world's most contested piece of land, both Israel and Palestine commonly refer to the region bounded by the Mediterranean Sea to the west, Jordan to the east, Lebanon and Syria to the north and Egypt to the south (Milton-Edwards & Farrell, 2013). Both ideologies express complicated *primal mourning* and preserve infantile omnipotence (Racamier, 1989). Both deny the kinship and interdependence of their peoples as siblings in this region, and both allow siblings to avoid being seen simultaneously as victims and perpetrators (Kaës, 2014). This atmosphere of idealisation and grandiosity is a common feature of *incestuality*.

To feel secure and regain their *primary narcissism*, the Palestinian group, operating at a pre-genital level, organised itself around revered and idolised leaders. Palestinians idealised leaders such as Sheikh Yassin, who founded Hamas, and Sheikh al-Qassam, who waged a holy war against the British colonialists and their allies in the 1930s. For Palestinians, these idolised leaders seem to have replaced their ego-deal (Freud, 1921) and the *psychic envelope* that their nation-state fails to provide. These leaders resemble the primal fathers of the primitive horde, who invested their narcissism in a phallic defence against the horror of castration and the recognition of kinship, even if it meant neglecting the establishment of a symbolic order (Kaës, 2016). The role of the tyrant, a self-proclaimed pseudo-father, replaced the symbolic role of the father. Sheikhs Qassam and Yassin may have been seen as representing an early primal father, such as Saladin, who triumphed over the Crusaders in AD 1187. Indeed, in its 1988 charter, Hamas refers to its religious ancestors rather than its homeland and its constitutional law of reason, perhaps reflecting the problematic kinship of the Palestinian people to their newly defined territorial motherland.

The majority of the Palestinian community, especially in the Gaza Strip, showed their loyalty to Hamas, its beliefs and its revered leaders during the 2006 Palestinian legislative elections. This loyalty gave them a false sense of containment, security and well-being. The Palestinian group thus demonstrated the basic assumption mentality dependency (Bion, 1961). According to Hopper (2009) and Hopper and Weinberg (2018), it regressed to functioning as a fused and confused mass under the aegis of the massification pole of the basic assumption mentality incohesion: aggregation/massification, whereby the group functions as either an individualistic aggregate or a fusional and confusional mass. Massification often leads to a fervent idealisation of the group and its leader and a strong identification with both the idolised leader and individual group members. It often reflects a desire to merge with a maternal, imagined mind and body (Hopper, 2009). For Palestinians, the ideological group Hamas appears to have become an idealised mother figure or 'good breast' that heals their narcissistic wounds (Chasseguet-Smirgel, 1985). Unlike its secular rivals, Hamas offers its supporters a new sense of identity centred on victory and devotion to God. Its ultimate goal is the revival of the Islamic Ummah or nation (Milton-Edwards & Farrell, 2013). In their loyalty to Hamas, Palestinians seem to be trying to recover their *primary narcissism* in a new version of the ego ideal (Freud, 1914) and a *closing ideology*. They seem to have merged with each other and with their leader, their land and their ideals (Chasseguet-Smirgel, as cited in Ostow, 1996). Their ideologies of entitlement (Volkan, 2007) became characterised by the dream of reclaiming all the lost lands currently occupied by others.

Hamas has grown steadily since its inception due to the lack of progress on Palestinian rights. It has become a major player in the Arab and Palestinian-Israeli conflicts, as well as in the political Islamic field in the region. At the Palestinian level, Hamas has maintained its popularity through military action, educational and social programmes, charitable initiatives and religious teachings, which have enabled it to win the support of Palestinians both inside and outside Palestine. Moreover, as the PLO's legitimacy and popularity declined, Hamas gained momentum, winning local, student and trade union elections in the West Bank and Gaza (Hroub, 2010).

In the late 1980s, during the First Intifada, Hamas emerged as a new player in the Palestinian political landscape with the aim of transforming the long-standing conflict between Palestinians and Israel. Its motivation stemmed from the belief in the righteousness of its cause, driven by its religious obligation to establish a Palestinian state where citizens could fulfil their duty as servants of God. This differed from the more secular nationalist perspective of the PLO under Yasser Arafat. Hamas claimed that its nationalism was unwavering and pure, in contrast to that of the PLO (Jefferis, 2016).

In line with *incestual* dynamics, the Palestinian people coped with their community's traumatic experiences, complicated separation and individuation, feelings of shame and humiliation, and archaic anxieties by unconsciously engaging in paranoid-schizoid splitting (Klein, 1958). A paranoid-schizoid Palestinian ideology emerged as a coping mechanism, but also as an enactment of the fragile ego state of the Palestinian collective and its group dynamics. The Palestinian Messiah, Hamas, emerged to define the Palestinian body envelope and consolidate Palestinian identity. Hamas thus introduced a method of legitimate resistance that combined religion, nationalism and resistance into a powerful and successful mix. As an opposition movement, Hamas achieved significant results that were well received by many Palestinians (Jefferis, 2016).

Hamas was seen as a movement promising 'liberation, pride and dignity', while the PLO's approach of negotiating with Israel was seen as accepting a 'life of humiliation' under occupation. The conflict between these two groups, which originally began in the 1970s and 1980s under the Brotherhood, had become a struggle for the future of Palestinian nationalism and identity. A fraternal pact governed by the unconscious dynamics of a symbolic *fraternal complex* could not structure an alliance between Palestinian siblings. The interplay of hatred, envy and jealousy, on the one hand, and love, ambivalence and identification with the other sibling, on the other, characteristic of the symbolic and *Oedipal fraternal complex*, was split under the aegis of the archaic version of the *fraternal complex* (Kaës, 2008). Thus, although Fatah and the PLO recognised the limitations of armed struggle and turned to peaceful tactics between 1959 and 1988, Hamas did not see this as relevant and opted for a strategy of jihad in the struggle for Palestinian liberation. It believed that its Islamic values would give it the strength to overcome the challenges that had hampered the PLO in the past.

Throughout the 1990s, Hamas opposed the PLO's attempts to resolve the conflict with Israel peacefully and politically. The Palestinian siblings could not establish a viable fraternal pact that was based on the fundamental prohibitions of incest, cannibalism and murder (Kaës, 2014), nor could they accept the 'law of the mother' (Mitchell, 2006, 2013a, 2013b, 2014). By claiming that Palestine was an Islamic waqf, or religious trust, Hamas undermined the PLO's moral authority to negotiate land for peace with Israel. Moreover, Hamas's refusal to trust Israel's promises meant that any agreements reached by the PLO were subject to Palestinian suspicion. In addition, Hamas actively supported violent attacks against Israeli citizens, thus undermining the PLO's credibility as a voice for Palestine because it lacked the power to stop the violence the Israelis wanted (Jefferis, 2016).

The collapse of the peace process in the 1990s and the increasing violence of Israeli repression caused Palestinians to lose hope in the possibility of reaching a peaceful agreement with Israel. Disillusionment with negotiations contributed to the decline of the Fatah movement, which had been the main proponent of the 1993 Oslo Accords. In addition, the mismanagement and corruption of the Fatah-led PA played a crucial role in the electoral success of Hamas. The Palestinian people were dissatisfied with the PA's failure to deliver basic services. The rise of Hamas also posed a challenge to Fatah, the leading force in the PLO and the dominant party in Palestinian society (Hroub, 2010). In paranoid-schizoid functioning, the Palestinian siblings were thus split into the righteous Hamas and the corrupt Fatah, and only the righteous should rule.

After the failure of the Camp David summit in 2000, Hamas saw its rise and expansion as a divine intervention that sabotaged diplomatic efforts (Baconi, 2018). With infantile omnipotence, it metaphorically embodied a Messiah who would save the Palestinian collective from succumbing to what they perceived as alienating and degrading pacts. Hamas's decision to launch the 7 October 2023 attacks on the 50th anniversary of the 1973 Yom Kippur War may have been intended to recall the temporary unity of the Sunni Muslim Arab states following the victories of Syria and Egypt against Israel in the early stages of the Yom Kippur War (Meyer, 2024) and to instil pride in their people and deliver them from the feelings of impotence, shame and humiliation.

However, in an unconscious compulsion of repetition, Hamas's 7 October attack risks driving the Palestinian people of Gaza into Egypt's Sinai desert. Paradoxically, Hamas, the saviour, has mutated into the scapegoat responsible for Palestinian displacement and humiliation. As I argued in Chapter 4, the Israeli-Palestinian conflict seems to have revived the biblical and Koranic narratives of the complicated relationship between Abraham, Sarah and Hagar, and the sibling rivalry between their two sons, Isaac and Ishmael. Abraham's decision to give in to pressure from his wife Sarah to banish his elder son Ishmael and his mother Hagar to the desert to protect her son Isaac from his unruly half-brother may have contributed to the sense of shame and victimhood felt by Muslims, Arabs and Palestinians.

The alleged intervention of God in the failed peace process may be an unconscious sign of redemption for Hamas, who, as God's Messiah, can finally undo the effects of Abraham's decision to exile Ishmael and his mother Hagar. However, the aftermath of Hamas's 7 October 2023 attack threatens to repeat the same biblical decision. In driving their Palestinian siblings to the borders of the Egyptian Sinai desert, the Israelis also seem to be unconsciously re-enacting the trauma of their exodus, projecting it onto their Palestinian siblings.

In 2006, Hamas won the Palestinian legislative elections, replacing Fatah as the dominant group and highlighting the lack of popularity of the PLO leadership. It promised to form a government free of corruption and to support the Palestinian right to armed resistance against the Israeli occupation. The group has drawn support from radical Islamic fundamentalists who believe that Israel and the international community have denied them the right to a state of their own. This message also resonates with the countless Palestinian refugees who live in impoverished conditions and long to return to the land they or their ancestors were forced to flee in 1948 when Israel was created. Residents of the West Bank and Gaza suffer dire living conditions as a result of both the Israeli occupation and the neglect of a corrupt Palestinian government. This has created a vacuum that Hamas has filled (Levitt, 2006).

Through its non-military branches, Hamas provides essential services such as food, healthcare, education and other social services, which has contributed to its success. Although Hamas was officially founded in 1987, its founders and predecessors had been building a grassroots network of charitable and social activities for decades. This network has now become a shadow government that rivals the services provided by the official PA, the United Nations and humanitarian agencies. The appeal of Hamas lies in its religious ideology, which promotes the unity of the faithful umma. This explains how it emerged victorious in the 2006 legislative elections while Fatah was defeated (Milton-Edwards & Farrell, 2013).

Hamas thus presents two faces to the world at once, like the two-faced god Janus of Greek mythology. One face is visible through its involvement in 'charitable' organisations that provide social services. The other face can be seen in Gaza, where Hamas has committed terrorist acts against military and civilian targets in its commitment to eliminate the state of Israel from the Middle East (Freedman, 2019). However, Hamas may be the *scapegoat*/Messiah (Houzel & Catoire, 1994), playing the dual role of holding its fragmented nation-state together and bearing the burden of being its disruptive agent. It may have become the *identified patient* and symptom of the Palestinian unconscious dynamics of complicated individuation.

Following its successful participation in the Palestinian legislative elections, Hamas was faced with the challenge of governing. Its previous tactics proved ineffective as it now had to act like a state while still being labelled a terrorist group. This caused major problems as they were ill-equipped to meet the basic needs of the people they represented, leading to a decline in their popularity. Their inability to control the use of force on their territory severely hampers their ability to negotiate an end to the blockade of Gaza. Moreover, their failure to persuade other violent groups on their territory to join such negotiations has led to doubts about their legitimacy as a resistance movement. The Arab Spring has also left a deep-seated mistrust between Islamist opposition groups and the governments they oppose (Jefferis, 2016). Thus, despite the face of the Messiah, the saviour, that Hamas presents, it is also the scapegoat, the fanatical ideological organisation that terrorises its people, its neighbours and the international community. It must therefore be sacrificed, like a scapegoat, to bring peace to the Palestinian people. Hamas thus bears the burden of being the breaking force of the Palestinian people and of their failed peace efforts.

Having seized control of the Gaza Strip from its rival Palestinian sibling, Fatah, in 2007, Hamas, has since ruled independently of the Palestinian

National Authority, enacting the *archaic fraternal complex* with the unconscious phantasy of returning to the womb and becoming the exclusive owner of the mother's space and her phallus. The strained relationship between Hamas and Fatah has led to failed attempts at cooperation and calls for the dissolution of the PA. More recently, there have been calls for change within the PLO, and the Hamas-Fatah reconciliation agreement and the establishment of an interim unity government are seen as steps in this direction. However, a key concern remains whether Hamas, if it were to join the PLO, would honour current agreements with Israel, and whether the international community would accept the inclusion of Hamas and other resistance organisations in the PLO (Passia, 2014).

Final remarks

Although Hamas initially sought to create an Islamic state encompassing the whole of British-mandated Palestine, it eventually agreed with Fatah in 2005, 2006 and 2007 to accept the 1967 borders. In 2017, Hamas updated its charter to endorse the creation of a Palestinian state on the 1967 borders, while continuing to deny Israel's existence. In the light of the ongoing Israeli-Palestinian conflict, Hamas has extended an offer to Israel for a long-lasting ceasefire, known as a hudna. This proposal, originally made by Sheikh Yassin in the 1990s, includes the condition of a sovereign state in the areas of the West Bank, Gaza and East Jerusalem that have been under Israeli occupation since the 1967 war. Hamas leaders continue to reiterate this offer to demonstrate their flexibility in response to evolving situations (Milton-Edwards & Farrell, 2013).

Since 2006, however, scholars have warned against Hamas's claims that it seeks a long-term ceasefire and peaceful coexistence with Israel (Alsoos, 2021). They argue that agreeing to the proposed long-term hudna, which includes a Palestinian state on the 1967 borders, would not lead to peace with Israel. Instead, Hamas's ultimate project remains the liberation of 'historic Palestine' and the creation of an Islamic state encompassing all of former British-mandated Palestine. In this vision, Jewish citizens would have the right to live as members of a community, but not as an independent Jewish state. The authors warn against Hamas's belief that it will eventually have enough influence to reclaim all of Palestine and suggest that agreeing to a Palestinian state in the West Bank and Gaza as part of a ceasefire agreement would only provide a temporary solution without recognition of Israel. However, other experts (Ravid, 2008) believe that Hamas would in fact be implicitly recognising the existence of Israel.

Following Hamas's aggressive attack on 7 October 2023, many Israelis who previously believed in Hamas's political evolution since 2017, when it published its revised charter outlining its principles and policies, are now questioning their beliefs (Klein 2024).

Hamas argues that, to move forward after the conflict, it is necessary to hold elections in which it will participate in a demilitarised or indirect way. Hamas insists that any plan that excludes it will be unworkable (Klein, 2024). According to Klein (2024), the recently revived two-state solution could serve as a compromise for both sides to achieve peace and reconstruction in Gaza. Hamas has shown its willingness to be part of the political institutions established by the Oslo Accords, and rather than excluding it, it would be more beneficial to ask it to fulfil its obligations, just as Israel will be expected to do.

If, as I have argued in this chapter, Hamas's ideological stance is indeed an expression of the complicated Palestinian process of separation and individuation, and if it emerges as a response to Palestinian narcissistic injuries, feelings of impotence, shame, humiliation and misery, then the establishment of a Palestinian nation-state with clear and viable geographical borders or body envelope becomes crucial to the creation of an integrated self or national identity. A dismembered body envelope that the 1967 borders might create, in the absence of a strong connection between the West Bank and the Gaza Strip, would only perpetuate the psychic fragmentation of the Palestinian people and lead to the compulsive repetition of violence in search of self-integration. A viable body envelope would help to establish law and order, transforming the defensive ideology of the Palestinian people into a system of values that can better structure their lives. The Palestinian collective can abandon the armed struggle or lesser jihad in favour of the inner or 'greater' jihad, which requires a struggle against one's own instincts and desires. The Palestinian people can deal with their narcissistic injuries, overcome their feelings of shame and humiliation and let go of their phantasy of returning to the British-mandated Palestinian womb. A viable body envelope can also help them to renounce infantile omnipotence and the desire to be the sole owners of the space of mother 'historic Palestine' and its phallus.

However, to establish an independent Palestinian nation-state with defined borders, the Israeli sibling must also recognise the legitimacy of the Palestinian sibling's needs and agree to share the same motherland. Both the Israeli and Palestinian siblings must abandon their closing ideologies and accept their symbolic castration, renouncing the phantasy of total possession of their motherland. It is necessary for both parties to come to terms with their sibling traumas (Mitchell, 2006, 2013a, 2013b, 2014) and accept the 'law of the mother'. As a result, they can renounce the re-enactment of their respective biblical and Koranic narratives of Abraham, his wives—Sarah and Hagar—and his sons—Isaac and Ishmael—and dissociate themselves from their mutual identification with the primal father Abraham who banished his own son. The unconscious fratricidal phantasies of the *archaic fraternal complex* that drives their relations can be contained and symbolised. For both Israelis and Palestinians, the Israelis would no longer be just Isaac, and the Palestinians no longer the exiled recalcitrant Ishmael.

References

Alsoos, I. (2021). From jihad to resistance: The evolution of Hamas's discourse in the framework of mobilization. *Middle Eastern Studies, 57*(5): 1–22.

Baconi, T. (2018). *Hamas contained: The rise and pacification of Palestinian resistance* (Kindle edition). Stanford, CA: Stanford University Press.

Ben-Dror, E. (2007). The Arab struggle against partition: The international arena of summer 1947. *Middle Eastern Studies, 43*(2): 259–293. https://doi.org/10.1080/00263200601114117.

Benghozi, P. (2016). Clinique identitaire de la radicalisation idéologique et Djihad dans les organisations incestueuses et incestuelles [An identity-based clinical approach to ideological radicalisation in incestuous and incestual organisations]. *Revue de Psychothérapie Psychanalytique de Groupe, 67*(2): 51–66.

Bion, W. R. (1961). *Experiences in groups and other papers.* London: Tavistock. https://doi.org/10.4324/9780203359075

Brenner, I. (2009). The Palestinian/Israeli conflict: A geopolitical identity disorder. *American Journal of Psychoanalysis, 69*(1): 62–71. https://doi.org/10.1057/ajp.2008.42

Britannica, T. Editors of Encyclopaedia. (2024). *Israel-Hamas war. Encyclopedia Britannica.* Retrieved from https://www.britannica.com/event/Israel-Hamas-War

Chasseguet-Smirgel, J. (1985). The ego ideal and the psychology of groups. *Free Associations 1, 2*: 31–60.

Freedman, I. (2019). *Hamas: The story of Islamic Jihad on Israel's front lines* (Civilization Jihad reader series book 14) (Kindle edition). Washington, DC: The Center for Security Policy Press.

Freud, S. (1914). On narcissism. In: J. Strachey (Ed.), *The standard edition of the complete psychological works of Sigmund Freud, Volume XIV (1914–1916): On the history of the psycho-analytic movement, papers on metapsychology and other works* (pp. 67–102). London: The Hogarth Press.

Freud, S. (1921). Group psychology and the analysis of the ego. In: J. Strachey (Ed.), *The standard edition of the complete psychological works of Sigmund Freud, Volume XVIII (1920–1922): Beyond the pleasure principle* (pp. 65–144). London: The Hogarth Press.

Hopper, E. (2009). The theory of the basic assumption of incohesion: Aggregation/massification or (BA) I: A/M. *British Journal of Psychotherapy, 25*: 214–229.

Hopper, E., & Weinberg, H. (2018). *The social unconscious in persons, groups and societies: Mainly theory.* The new international library of group analysis book (Kindle edition., Vol. 1). London & New York: Routledge.

Houzel, D., & Catoire, G. (1994). *La Famille comme Institution [The family as an institution].* Paris: Apsygée.

Hroub, K. (2010). *Hamas: A beginner's guide* (Kindle edition). London: Pluto Press.

Jefferis, J. (2016). *Hamas: Terrorism, governance, and its future in Middle East politics* (Praeger security international) (Kindle edition). Santa Barbara, CA: Bloomsbury Publishing.

Kaës, R. (2008). *Le Complexe Fraternel [The fraternal complex].* Paris: Dunod.

Kaës, R. (2014). *Les Alliances Inconscientes [Unconscious alliances].* Paris: Dunod. https://doi.org/10.3917/dunod.kaes.2014.01

Kaës, R. (2016). *L'idéologie, l'idéal, l'idée, l'idole [The ideology, the ideal, the idea, the idol].* Paris: Dunod. https://doi.org/10.3917/dunod.kaese.2016.01

Kancyper, L. (2011). Exploring core concepts: Sexuality, dreams and the unconscious. *International Journal of Psychoanalysis, 92*(2): 265–267.

Kernberg, O. F. (2003). Sanctioned social violence: A psychoanalytic view-Part I. *International Journal of Psycho-Analysis, 84*(3): 683–698. https://doi. org/10.1516/002075703766644913

Klein, M. (1958). On the development of mental functioning. *International Journal of Psycho-Analysis, 39*(2–4): 84–90.

Klein, M. (1996). Competing brothers: The web of Hamas-PLO relations. *Terrorism and Political Violence, 8*(2), 111–132.

Klein, M. (2024). Hamas's narrative of 7 October and the impossibility of ignoring it. *Instituto Affari Internationali (IAI) Commentaries, 24/05*. Retrieved from https://www. iai.it/en/pubblicazioni/hamass-narrative-7-october-and-impossibility-ignoring-it

Levitt, M. (2006). *Hamas: Politics, charity, and terrorism in the service of Jihad* (Kindle edition). New Haven & London: Yale University Press.

McKernan, B., Michaelson, R., Graham-Harrison, E., Kierszenbaum, Q., Balousha, H., Taha, S., Sherwood, H., & Beaumont, P. (2023). *Seven days of terror that shook the world and changed the Middle East.* Retrieved from https://www.theguardian. com/world/2023/oct/14/seven-days-of-terror-that-shook-the-world-and-changed-th e-middle-east

Meyer, E. D. (2024). *A second Nakba or a great day of return? (The Palestinian question before and after the Israel-Hamas war).* Retrieved from https://www.researchgate.net/publication/380490918_A_Second_Nakba_or_a_Great_Day_of_ Return_The_Palestinian_Question_Before_and_After_the_Israel-Hamas_War/ link/663ee9b706ea3d0b7458d275/download?_tp=eyJjb250ZXh0Ijp7ImZpcnN0UG FnZSI6InB1YmxpY2F0aW9uIiwicGFnZSI6InB1YmxpY2F0aW9uIn19

Milton-Edwards, B., & Farrell, S. (2013). *Hamas: The Islamic resistance movement* (Kindle edition). Cambridge: Polity Press.

Mitchell, J. (2006). From infant to child: The sibling trauma, the rite de passage, and the construction of the 'Other' in the social group. *Fort Da, 12*: 35–49.

Mitchell, J. (2013a). Siblings: Thinking theory. *Psychoanalytic Study of the Child, 67*: 14–34.

Mitchell, J. (2013b). The law of the mother: Sibling trauma and the brotherhood of war. *Canadian Journal of Psychoanalysis, 21*: 145–159.

Mitchell, J. (2014). Siblings and the psychosocial. *Organizational and Social Dynamics, 14*: 1–12.

Ostow, M. (1996). Myth and madness: A report of a psychoanalytic study of antisemitism. *International Journal of Psycho-Analysis, 77*(1): 15–31.

Palestinian Academic Society for the Study of International Affairs - Passia. (2014). *PLO VS PA.* Retrieved from http://passia.org/media/filer_public/8a/ e7/8ae7c030-ac1d-4688-b3f4-606fbd50cd41/pa-plo2.pdf

Racamier, P. C. (1989). *Antœdipe et ses Destins [Antoedipus and its destinies].* Paris: Apsygée.

Racamier, P. C. (1992). *Le Génie des Origines [The genius of origins].* Paris: Payot and Rivage.

Racamier, P. C. (1995). *L'inceste et l'incestuel [The incest and the incestual].* Paris: Éditions du Collège.

Ravid, B. (2008). *In 2006 letter to Bush, Haniyeh offered compromise with Israel.* Retrieved from   https://www.haaretz.com/print-edition/news/in-2006-letter-to-bush-haniyeh-offered-compromise-with-israel-1.257213). *Haaretz.* Archived (https://web.archive.

org/web/201511252 15124/https://www.haaretz.com/print-edition/news/in-2006-letter-to-bush-haniyeh-offered-compromise-with-israel-1.257213) from the original on 25 November 2015.

United Nations News: Global Perspective Human Stories. (2018). *US resolution to condemn activities of Hamas voted down in General Assembly.* Retrieved from https://news.un.org/en/story/2018/12/1027881

United Nations Office for the Coordination of Humanitarian Affairs. (2023). *Fact sheet: Israel and Palestine* (9 October 2023). (Press Release). Retrieved from https://reliefweb.int/report/occupied-palestinian-territory/fact-sheet-israel-and-palestine-conflict-9-october-2023

Volkan, V. D. (2004). *Blind trust: Large groups and their leaders in times of crisis and terror.* Charlottesville, VA: Pitchstone Publishing.

Volkan, V. D. (2007). Not letting go: From individual perennial mourners to societies with entitlement ideologies. In: F. Glocer Fiorini, S. Lewkowicz, & T. Bokanowski (Eds.), *On Freud's mourning and melancholia* (pp. 90–109). London: International Psychoanalytic Association.

Volkan, V. D. (2013). Large-group-psychology in its own right: Large-group identity and peace-making. *International Journal of Applied Psychoanalytic Studies, 10*(3): 210–246. https://doi.org/10.1002/aps.1368

Chapter 6

Reflections on national and international dialogues

Social traumas are the building blocks of the social unconscious of societies, organisations and groups. They include repressed, denied, split-off and disavowed aspects of traumatising social realities and their internal representations. Social traumas can lead to the collapse and disintegration of the group envelope (Anzieu, 1984). They can trigger annihilation, fear and isomorphic defences, leading to totalitarian societies and ideologies.

To protect themselves from the intolerable effects of social trauma and to freeze the traumatic elements of their experience, individuals may collectively deny the cause and responsibility of social violence or minimise its impact (Kaës, 2014). They may also collectively sever their affective ties to the immediate past (Mitscherlich & Mitscherlich, 1975), erasing memories of social trauma and painful shared affects. As a result, these memories are encapsulated in social-psychic retreats within groups, organisations and societies, such as enclaves and ghettos (Hopper & Weinberg, 2018). These social-psychic retreats are similar to black holes (Doron, 2018).

Through these pathological defences, traumatised individuals collectively avoid mourning (Hopper & Weinberg, 2018; Kaës, 2014; Mitscherlich & Mitscherlich, 1975). Their repressed and denied material generates intolerable affects such as guilt and shame, as well as fears of annihilation and separation (Doron, 2018; Mitscherlich & Mitscherlich, 1975). However, social-psychic retreats generate enactment and traumatophilia as a compulsion to repeat (Hopper & Weinberg, 2018). Individuals collectively re-enact and recreate traumatic experiences through projective and introjective identification processes. Time collapses (Volkan, 2004, 2013) and new and later situations are seen as equivalent to old and earlier ones (Hopper, 2003).

Trauma work

To stop the cycle of violence that has trapped them for more than a century, parties to conflicts, especially violent and intractable ones, must engage in trauma work (Asséo & Dreyfus-Asséo, 2014). Trauma work is a psychic work

DOI: 10.4324/9781003545842-8

of mourning that restores the sense of time and reconnects the immediate experience with the past and the future. It can help conflict parties to work through their unconscious group dynamics and the traumatic elements of their group history that underlie their intractable conflicts; to confront their archaic anxieties, unbearable affects and death and murder phantasies; to appropriate their projected parts and to mourn past traumas. In addition, trauma work can help them overcome their social-psychic retreats, which are often the '"hidden destructive rulers" behind chronic resistance to change and obstacles to social healing processes' (Hopper & Weinberg, 2018, p. 230).

As a result, the parties to violent conflicts are better able to work through their centuries-old traumas, feelings of shame, humiliation, resentment and remorse. Their *fraternal complex* (Kaës, 2008), an unconscious intrapsychic triangular organisation (ego-mother/father-sibling) that regulates relationships on a horizontal level, as opposed to the Oedipal complex that regulates relationships on a vertical axis (ego-mother-father), would then change from the archaic and talionic 'eye for an eye' system of retribution to the symbolic and Oedipal (Kaës, 2008), allowing for ambivalence and an interplay between love and hate. The parties to conflict would be better able to renounce the unconscious pre-genital phantasies of returning to the mother's womb and aspiring to be her phallus and the exclusive owner of her space, which is the central phantasy of the *archaic fraternal complex* (Kaës, 2008). They would be more able to move from a paranoid-schizoid to a depressive position (Klein, 1958). The embittered warring parties can thus abandon their victimhood and their demands for retribution and punishment. They can acknowledge their dual position as victims and executioners so that they can mourn what they have done to each other over the years, face their anxieties and feelings of guilt and shame, reconcile and then break the cycle of violence. Only then will they be able to overcome their fratricidal phantasies, identify with the similar other of the same generation and reach a pact for a new social order in which differences are recognised and respected, while brothers are seen as equals and people with whom cooperation and solidarity are possible.

Through the psychic work of *primal mourning* (Racamier, 1992), the warring Lebanese sectarian sub-groups and the Israelis and Palestinians can symbolically separate themselves from the maternal body, which itself is recognised as different from the siblings. Lebanese, Israelis and Palestinians would mourn the desire for symbiosis and total possession of the object. They would be better able to abandon the archaic phantasy of returning to the womb, accepting symbolic castration and identifying with the mother who gives birth. Separation would become possible and would no longer take the form of tearing. They would no longer perceive their siblings as part objects. They would renounce their incestuous desires, overcome their hatred and aggression towards their siblings, agree to share the maternal space of their nation-state and find in each other acceptable figures of identification.

Lebanese, Israelis and Palestinians would be better able to define their bodily envelopes, allowing them to distinguish the Me from the not-Me. They would demarcate clear boundaries to form autonomous ego-nation-states. With clear boundaries demarcated, the warring siblings would renounce phallic phantasies of omnipotence, accept the symbolic castration of their nation, acknowledge their kinship and establish a symbolic order. They would be better able to access secondary narcissism, which refers to an objectal stage of differentiation and implies the recognition of otherness and of the object as external and independent. Their parts are unified into a total object, that is, mature, independent ego-nation-states. The warring parties can all identify with the symbolic father and envisage a symbolic order that does not depend on a *closing ideological position* and a *scapegoat/messiah*. They can seal a new fraternal pact under the aegis of the law of reason, fraternal equality and mutual respect.

Final remarks

For transformation to be effective, national and international dialogues must help the parties to the conflict to do the psychic work of mourning. However, most diplomatic efforts have focused on rational analyses of real interests, and despite extensive negotiations and dialogue, the parties have failed to achieve sustainable peace. In Lebanon, national and inter-Lebanese dialogues have served to break political deadlocks, address issues of national concern that divide the country and reopen channels of communication between Lebanon's warring siblings. However, these dialogues have been ineffective in resolving core issues (Wählisch, 2017), and the Lebanese ego-state has remained paralysed, unable to exercise its executive, legislative and judicial functions, while its institutions have been infiltrated by bureaucratic corruption. For Israelis and Palestinians, years of deadlocked negotiations and violent conflict have left both sceptical about the possibility of resolving their dispute (Jarrar, 2010). Thus, for any national dialogue to be productive, mediators must be aware of the unconscious dynamics affecting the mediating group, its individual participants and their intersubjective relationships.

An international process of negotiation between the twins, Lebanon and Syria, and their nephew/niece, Israel, born later from the womb of their sibling, that is, the British-mandated Palestine, must help the twins to mourn the original state of fusion that resulted from being held as part objects in the body and psychic space of the mother, the Ottoman Empire. These countries must mourn the desire to regain the illusion of a magical, omnipotent and inseparable brotherhood united by *primary narcissism* (Freud, 1914), which refers to a historically objectless stage of undifferentiation that precedes object recognition; otherwise, they will continue to go to war as part objects linked by envious rivalry and archaic identifications (Kaës, 2008). International negotiations must help these countries to work through their sibling complex and accept the irreversible narcissistic injury of their inability to perpetuate themselves as narcissistic doubles. This is fundamental to the building of distinct identities and the democratic rule of law. In Latin, rivalry refers to neighbours competing for the same stream (rivus) and their right to share it. However, in addition to the desire for access to the object, sibling rivalry also implies the projection of denied parts of the self. International negotiations must therefore help the sibling countries to reappropriate these parts of themselves to tolerate ambivalence towards the other nation, while accepting it as a total object that is at once different and similar.

In the context of peacemaking and peacebuilding, especially in the context of civil wars, mediators must be alert to issues of *primary narcissism*, body and *psychic envelopes*, pregenital modes of functioning, primitive anxieties, archaic manifestations of the *fraternal complex*, unconscious pathological alliances and fraternal pacts as they unfold through transference and counter-transference dynamics during the peacemaking and peacebuilding processes, so as to assist mediation groups in moving from a basic assumption mentality to a work group mentality (Bion, 1961) and from a paranoid-schizoid position to a depressive position (Klein, 1958). Emerging feelings of guilt and grief and a desire for reparation will allow the siblings to tolerate their ambivalence and transform their conflicts, which will then promote integration and cooperation within the group.

In Part II, I develop a group psychoanalytic approach to peacemaking and peacebuilding practices.

References

Asséo, R., & Dreyfus-Asséo, S. (2014). Deuil dans la culture l'actuel, détail par détail [Mourning in culture today, detailed by detail Mourning in culture]. *Revue Française de Psychanalyse, 78*(5): 1265–1335. https://doi.org/10.3917/rfp.785.1263

Anzieu, D. (1984). *The group and the unconscious.* London: Routledge & Kegan Paul.

Bion, W. R. (1961). *Experiences in groups and other papers.* London: Tavistock. https://doi.org/10.4324/9780203359075

Doron, Y. (2018). 'Black holes' as a collective defence against shared fears of annihilation in a small therapy group and in its contextual society. In: E. Hopper & H. Weinberg (Eds.), *The social unconscious in persons, groups and societies: The foundation matrix extended and reconfigured.* The new international library of group analysis book 3 (Kindle edition., pp. 151–162). London & New York: Routledge.

Freud, S. (1914). On narcissism. In: J. Strachey (Ed.), *The standard edition of the complete psychological works of Sigmund Freud, Volume XIV (1914–1916): On the history of the psycho-analytic movement, papers on metapsychology and other works* (pp. 67–102). London: The Hogarth Press.

Hopper, E. (2003). *The social unconscious: Selected papers (International library of group analysis book 22)* (Kindle edition). Philadelphia, PA: Jessica Kingsley Publishers.

Hopper, E., & Weinberg, H. (2018). *The social unconscious in persons, groups and societies: Mainly theory*. The new international library of group analysis book (Kindle edition., Vol. 1). London & New York: Routledge.

Jarrar, A. (2010). Palestinian suffering: Some personal, historical, and psychoanalytic reflections. *International Journal of Applied Psychoanalytic Studies, 7*(3): 197–208. https://doi.org/10.1002/aps.252

Kaës, R. (2008). *Le Complexe Fraternel [The fraternal complex]*. Paris: Dunod.

Kaës, R. (2014). *Les Alliances Inconscientes [Unconscious alliances]*. Paris: Dunod. https://doi.org/10.3917/dunod.kaes.2014.01

Klein, M. (1958). On the development of mental functioning. *International Journal of Psycho-Analysis, 39*(2–4): 84–90.

Mitscherlich, A., & Mitscherlich, M. (1975). *The inability to mourn: Principles of collective behavior*. New York, NY: Grove Press.

Racamier, P. C. (1992). *Le Génie des Origines [The genius of origins]*. Paris: Payot and Rivage.

Volkan, V. D. (2004). *Blind trust: Large groups and their leaders in times of crisis and terror*. Charlottesville, VA: Pitchstone Publishing.

Volkan, V. D. (2013). Large-group-psychology in its own right: Large-group identity and peace-making. *International Journal of Applied Psychoanalytic Studies, 10*(3): 210–246. https://doi.org/10.1002/aps.1368

Wählisch, M. (2017). *The Lebanese national dialogue: Past and present experience of consensus-building. National dialogue handbook. Case studies*. Berlin: Berghof Foundation.

Part II

A group psychoanalytic device for peacemaking and peacebuilding

.

Chapter 7

Group psychoanalytic device and group psychoanalytic psychodrama

In this chapter, I will present a framework inspired by the work of the Cercles d'Études Françaises pour la Formation et la Recherche: Approche Psychanalytique du Groupe, du Psychodrame, de l'Institution (Circles of French Studies for Training and Research: Psychoanalytic Approach to the Group, to Psychodrama, to the Institution; CEFFRAP). In contrast to work in social psychology, and building on the work of Foulkes, Bion and Ezriel, among others, CEFFRAP studied the psychodynamics of small groups using verbal expression and psychodrama from a Freudian psychoanalytic perspective (Kaës et al., 2003; Kaës, 2000). Members interpret the unconscious individual and group psychic phenomena and their transferential dimensions, which remain largely unnoticed outside the psychoanalytic framework, although not without effect (Kaës et al., 2003). CEFFRAP has offered various modalities of psychoanalytic group work, including residential psychoanalytic group psychodrama seminars.

In general, psychoanalytic groups can be closed, in which the members remain constant from beginning to end; open, in which there are no restrictions on the entry and departure of members; and semi-open, in which places are filled according to the exit of participants' departures. Psychoanalytic verbal expression groups can be conducted face to face or back to back (Kaës, 2015). Each of these group types has its own particularities, indications, dynamics and effects.

Group psychoanalytic device

A group psychoanalytic device depends on a specific set of rules (Kaës, 2015) and has two functions. The paternal function defines the working laws of the group and limits the participants to talking and playing. It acts as an excitation barrier that favours symbolisation and transformation. The maternal function provides a holding environment (Winnicott, 1960) that contains, shapes and transforms its own emotional experiences and psychic reality, as well as those of its members and their intersubjective links.

DOI: 10.4324/9781003545842-10

The group thus provides a supportive experience. It provides a transitional or potential space—a space where the participants and the group as a whole feel safe enough to reveal and elaborate on the traumatic elements of their histories as they are revealed (through transference and enactment during the psychoanalytic process) so that they can be transformed and symbolised. With this psychoanalytic framework, a new field is created within which a new ongoing interactive link is formed, including unconscious elements (Baranger & Baranger, 2008). The new field, together with the unconscious group phantasies it generates, structures the psychoanalytic field, consciously and unconsciously influences its individual participants and produces the insight necessary to transform relationships.

The psychoanalysts leading the group announce these rules to launch group work. These rules define the temporal and spatial frameworks as well as the modalities of exchange and provide access to unconscious dynamics that might otherwise be inaccessible. It creates an asymmetry between participants and psychoanalysts that generates transference (Kaës et al., 2003). The enunciated framework distinguishes the psychoanalytic group from the life group by establishing the here and now of psychoanalytic work and the there and then of group life. The structure of sessions establishes a new and different world with its own specific boundaries, rules, founders and psychic functioning.

Regular group sessions of fixed duration and rhythm make it possible to reach the underlying archaic roots of the group's psychic apparatus. Psychoanalysts and participants meet only in group sessions. Psychoanalysts encourage participants to be diligent in attendance (the rule of regular attendance), associate freely, report what happens between sessions and respect confidentiality (the rule of discretion). The psychoanalysts listen with benevolent neutrality, that is, without judging, advising or pressuring the group towards a particular solution. They refrain from addressing the presenting problem and concentrate on uncovering the group's unconscious functioning.

Given the nature of the group sessions, the psychoanalysts state that they will not keep any secrets that a participant may wish to share privately; whatever needs to be shared must be shared with the group. Participants must respect the rule of abstinence, which requires that they refrain from using the group material in a perverted way to manipulate or discredit the group work or the participants. The rule of abstinence also applies to psychoanalysts, who must refrain from relationships with participants outside the sessions. This rule demarcates the inside and the outside—the psychoanalytic and the life space of the group. Any breach of these rules will be interpreted as an enactment to be analysed.

In this framework, the psychoanalysts see the group as an ensemble—an apparatus of psychic work (Kaës, 2000) with its own specific processes and effects that are irreducible to any constituent individual apparatus. In addition, the psychoanalysts listen to the psychic reality of the group as a whole as well as to its individual members and their intersubjective links. They also listen to intergroup dynamics, inter-organisational dynamics and societal dynamics. They interpret (1) participants' explicit discourse, (2) unconscious phantasies and transference/counter-transference in the group field and (3) participants' individual unconscious as expressions of group dynamics. The plurality of participants leads to a diffraction of psychic realities, each projecting and incorporating/identifying projectively.

Psychoanalysts analyse all group transferential expressions (Kaës, 2015): central, group, lateral, institutional, societal and inter-transferences. Central transference in the group refers to the participants' transference onto the psychoanalyst dyad, while group transference refers to the participants' transference onto the group as a whole as an object of representations and affects. Lateral transference refers to the participants' transference onto each other as fraternal imagoes, while institutional transference refers to their transference onto the institutions to which they belong and societal transference to their transference onto the outside world, which is often represented as tyrannical and threatening, but also as a place of hope for something better.

In this framework, the psychoanalysts pay attention to themselves as psychoanalysts, to their counter-transference and to their act of observation—the so-called meta-position (Kaës, 2015) specific to clinical observation. When psychoanalysts lead a group, they are simultaneously immersed as psychoanalysts while also separated as observers. They meet between sessions to elaborate on the group's experience and analyse their inter-transference; otherwise, group impasses occur and the potentiality of gaining insight and producing transformation is compromised. Inter-transference is both a manifestation of psychoanalysts' resistance to the psychoanalytic work and a way of understanding and releasing all the resistances manifesting in the group (Kaës, 2004).

In addition, group psychoanalysts observe and interpret the dynamics of the group. They observe psychic phenomena such as splitting, denial, identifications and projections. They observe group effects such as group illusion and breakage phantasies—phantasies that, when left unelucidated, lead to group impasses (Anzieu, 1984). Group psychoanalysts also observe phantasmatic resonance, which is the source of shared and common psychic functioning for each participant, and the expression of the re-actualisation of original phantasies (the return to the womb, seduction, the primal scene and castration). The participants organise themselves around the unconscious scenario of a member, with which their phantasies resonate. Psychoanalysts also listen to the group associative chain (Kaës, 2010, 2015), a speech delivered by several voices.

The psychoanalysts propose interpretations that address the group as a whole rather than giving individual interpretations. These group interpretations, as opposed to individual cures, are ahistorical in nature: psychoanalysts interpret the current unconscious desires, defences and anxieties that unfold in the here and now of the group experience without going back to their infantile origins (Ezriel, cited in Anzieu, 1984).

Group psychoanalysts see the group as analogous to dreams. Both deal with the same basic libidinal and aggressive drives. Both are imaginary accomplishments of repressed desires. The group is seen as having a common and shared dream space in which there is polyphony of dreaming, that is, intertwined dream processes and images that both reveal and influence the dynamics of the group as a whole, its members and their links (Kaës, 2002). The dreamer is both the subject of their own unconscious and a dream carrier for the group. Thus, when a group participant shares a dream, the group is dreaming collectively.

Participants often dream about conflicts and traumatic elements that cannot be addressed, explored or even thought about. Dreaming processes mentally indigestible traumatic experiences and translates them into dream thoughts that are useful for thinking (Bion, 1984). Thus, group psychoanalysts interpret the manifest content of the group experience to reveal its latent content. They help the group as a whole as well as its participants to explore the unconscious dynamics underlying their overt conflicts, repetitive relationship patterns and basic assumption mentality. This can lead to insights and effective group work that enable participants to work through the history of the group and its past traumas and their transgenerational transmission, so that the mourning process can be completed.

When the group cannot contain its internal tensions and feels threatened by them, it becomes defensive and resists transformation. It mobilises the basic assumption mentality (Bion, 1961), which interferes with the primary task the group wishes to accomplish and leads to psychic splitting and fragmentation of the group. The psychic apparatus of the group operates in an *incestual* mode (Racamier, 1995), whereby the group and its constituent members maintain a confusion of boundaries between the Me and the not-Me and are dominated by primary process thinking and enactments.

In such an environment, the group members may defensively idealise the group and its founders to find an identification for themselves. The group, then, functions according to the basic assumption mentality dependency (Bion, 1961), whereby the group organises itself around dependency on the idealised psychoanalysts as if they were to satisfy its needs. The group entertains the phantasy of omnipotence or narcissistic megalomania. Through this group illusion (Anzieu, 1984), the group counteracts its breakage phantasies—oral and phallic castration anxieties, paranoid anxieties of devouring and persecution, schizoid fragmentation anxieties and depressive separation anxieties.

To maintain a sense of megalomania, participants may unconsciously manipulate the psychoanalytic framework or discredit the psychoanalysts and the psychoanalytic process. With this perverse transference, participants create what psychoanalysts call a perverse group field, which can create an environment of mystification, ambiguity, paradoxicality and mediation dead-locks. *Perversity* is a defence against internal conflict and the universal psychic process of *primal mourning* (Racamier, 1992), which is at the origin of the differentiation and arrangement of object relationships. When a group avoids working through *primal mourning*, the autonomy and security of its members' self are threatened.

Group psychoanalytic psychodrama

Psychodrama can help participants to symbolise and transform their enactments and affects into thoughts. It can help them elaborate on their underlying unconscious dynamics, as diffracted in role-play scenes. Imagining play themes and staging them in a materialised play space creates an association of body, thought and affect. Playing is a symbolising and transformative act that is triggered by the associative verbal thread of the group. As with dreaming, playing activates primary process thinking (Kaës et al., 2003) and implies the mourning process. When impulses and drives are put into play, there is an implicit renunciation of their direct realisation. Moreover, the mobilisation of the body in play facilitates the expression and mentalisation of preverbal or proto-mental dynamics, which are a matrix of group basic-assumption mentalities and their related primitive emotional states (Bion, 1961). The most archaic levels of the psyche may not be accessible through verbal forms of expression. They are retained within the body and body-centred experiences (Gampel, 1993). Play is the double encounter of the intrapsychic and inter-subjective. Psychoanalysts see the play as staged by the group as a whole; it reveals what is at play in the group, the participants and their links.

In psychodrama, the spatio-temporal setting differs from that of verbal expression groups; the spatial structure changes from being circular to semi-circular. Two spaces are thus delineated: the space where participants sit with psychoanalysts/group animators and freely express themselves verbally and the empty space in the front of them, which becomes the area where the role-play takes place. Participants are thus oriented in a vector space from the back to the front—from the seating area to the play area—as in theatre (Kaës et al., 2003). In addition, the temporal structure is divided into three moments: the time for free verbal expression and elaboration of a play theme, the time for role-playing and the time for the elaboration of the role-play experience.

The psychoanalysts invite participants to share freely with the group. The emerging verbal material opens the field for participants to imagine and represent a scene. These scenarios develop from the personal associations of the participants and the associative thread of the group. The play takes place in the designated empty space and is characterised by injunctions of spontaneity and the rule of pretence, which trigger regression and provide access to archaic aspects of the group's psychic functioning. Roles are then chosen and distributed. If some participants choose not to play, they express themselves as witnesses. The scenario is then acted out. Eventually, the psychoanalysts stop the play, and the players return to their places in the semicircle. The psychoanalysts invite the participants to reflect on their play, interpreting the unconscious dynamics of the content of the staged scene. Thus, as with dreams, the play's manifest content is interpreted to reveal its latent content. This allows participants to gain insight. Furthermore, facilitating play is not only just about interpreting the latent content of play, be it the economy of the libido or the symbolism of desire, to explore archaic anxieties (Klein, 1955). It is about the experience of playing in itself, which leads to a transformation in one's relationship to oneself, to others and to the world (Winnicott, 1971). Volkan (2006) found that, during psycho-political dialogues, when participants symbolise and act out an anxiety-producing relationship, they gain insight and change their perceptions of each other.

Final remarks

A group psychoanalytic approach helps participants explore, elaborate on and symbolise the unconscious dynamics at play during their encounters to facilitate the transformation of their conflictual relationships. Group psychoanalysts analyse and interpret the psychic realities unfolding in the 'here and now' of the group experience, that is, the psychic realities of the group as a whole, its constituent members and their links. Such an approach can complement the current strategies of peacemakers and peacebuilders by helping participants to work through the unconscious dynamics at play during dialogues.

References

Anzieu, D. (1984). *The group and the unconscious*. London: Routledge & Kegan Paul.

Baranger, M., & Baranger, W. (2008). The analytic situation as a dynamic field. *The International Journal of Psychoanalysis*, *89*(4): 795–826. https://doi.org/10.1111/j.1745-8315.2008.00074.x

Bion, W. R. (1961). *Experiences in groups and other papers*. London: Tavistock. https://doi.org/10.4324/9780203359075

Bion, W. R. (1984). *Elements of psychoanalysis*. London: Karnac.

Gampel, Y. (1993). Access to the non-verbal through modelling in the psychoanalytic situation. *British Journal of Psychotherapy*, *9*(3): 280–290. https://doi.org/10.1111/j.1752-0118.1993.tb01227.x

Kaës, R. (2000). *L'appareil Psychique Groupal [The group psychic apparatus]*. Paris: Dunod.

Kaës, R. (2002). *La Polyphonie du Rêve: L'expérience Onirique Commune et Partagée [The polyphony of dreams: The common and shared oneric experience]*. Paris: Dunod.

Kaës, R. (2004). Intertransfert et analyse inter-transférentielle dans le travail psychanalytique conduit par plusieurs psychanalystes [Inter-transference and inter-transferential analysis in the psychoanalytic work led by several psychoanalysts]. *Filigrane*, *13*(2): 5–15.

Kaës, R. (2010). *La Parole et le Lien: Associativité et le Travail Psychique dans les Groups [The speech and the link: Associativity and psychic work in groups]*. Paris: Dunod.

Kaës, R. (2015). *L'extension de la Psychanalyse: Pour une Métapsychologie de Troisième Type [The extension of psychoanalysis: For a metapsychology of the third type]*. Paris: Dunod. https://doi.org/10.3917/dunod.kaes.2015.02

Kaës, R., Missenard, A., Nicolle, O., Benchimol, M., Blanchard, A.-M., Claquin, M., & Villier, J. (2003). *Le Psychodrame Psychanalytique de Groupe [Group psychoanalytic psychodrama]*. Paris: Dunod.

Klein, M. (1955). The psycho-analytic play technique: Its history and significance. In: M. Klein (Ed.), *The writings of Melanie Klein III: Envy and gratitude and other works* (pp. 1946–1963). London: Karnac.

Racamier, P. C. (1992). *Le Génie des Origines [The genius of origins]*. Paris: Payot and Rivage.

Racamier, P. C. (1995). *L'inceste et l'incestuel [The incest and the incestual]*. Paris: Éditions du Collège.

Volkan, V. D. (2006). *Killing in the name of identity: A study of bloody conflicts.* Charlottesville, VA: Pitchstone Publishing.

Winnicott, D. W. (1960). The theory of the parent–infant relationship. *International Journal of Psychoanalysis, 41:* 585–595.

Winnicott, D. W. (1971). *Playing and reality.* London: Tavistock Publications.

Chapter 8

A group psychoanalytic approach to peacemaking

Conflict is a natural expression of individual and group life. They are inherent in all human relationships and cannot be eliminated. They often create a dynamic balance with the capacity for change, adaptation and renewal. However, conflicts can become malignant and destructive, rewriting the history of relationships from a negative perspective. Moreover, all types of conflict in all types of relationships often reflect unconscious processes and may be symbolic of other hidden conflicts. The challenge is to transform the malignant expression of conflict into more benign and fruitful forms. Indeed, the conflict transformation approach, as opposed to the conflict resolution approach, seeks not only to manage or resolve a conflict but also to address its root causes (Galtung, 2000; Lederach, 2014; Miall, 2004).

Mediation and peacemaking

To manage, resolve and transform conflict, disputants often resort to mediation. Mediators tend to focus on analysing the contextual factors influencing the dispute, the mediation process and their roles and strategies as mediators; their approach remains rational and based on real interests, whether in regional, national or international conflicts. However, despite their efforts, mediators and peacemakers often find themselves locked in dialogues where irrationality prevails. Historical resentments and traumas can be reactivated, exacerbating existing conflicts, and ultimately contributing to stalemates in peacemaking efforts.

This has spurred mediators' interest in examining the psychological components influencing international relationships and mediation processes and outcomes, with Vamik Volkan among the pioneers. Volkan (1987, 1988, 1999a, 1999b, 2006, 2009, 2013, 2014) highlighted the primitive unconscious dynamics influencing sociopolitical conflicts and international relationships. However, despite Volkan's pioneering efforts to create a reflective space to promote psychologically informed dialogues, most psychoanalysts have limited their efforts to theoretical conceptualisations of international conflict. Less attention has been paid to applying a group psychoanalytic framework

DOI: 10.4324/9781003545842-11

to backchannel mediation and dialogues. However, such a framework could provide space for interpreting the unconscious dynamics underlying group processes.

Well-developed psychoanalytically oriented strategies, apart from a few such as those proposed by the International Dialogue Initiative (IDI) group, are still lacking in political mediation and dialogue. The IDI is a private, international, multidisciplinary group of psychoanalysts, academics, diplomats and other professionals who seek to understand and help overcome the psychological obstacles that impede the peaceful resolution of conflicts between communities, nations and cultures. Through reflective dialogue, the IDI seeks to promote mutual understanding between parties to conflict by exploring the historical and emotional roots of strained relationships, including the impact of past trauma on group identity. IDI develops effective strategies and interventions to gain insight into emotionally charged conflicts among large groups.

Among IDI members, Robi Friedman (2019) applied the 'Group Sandwich Model' to international conflict using large groups as a societal developmental space. In this model, Friedman sandwiched large group interaction, between two small group sessions to transform hatred into peaceful co-existence and reduce violence. Vamik Volkan, on the other hand, developed the Tree Model, which is a three-phase psychoanalytically informed interdisciplinary approach to unofficial diplomacy (1999b, 2006, 2011). The first phase involves psycho-political diagnosis of the conflictual situation; the second phase refers to psycho-political dialogues between high-level representatives of the opposing groups and the third phase implements a collaborative sociopolitical actions and governmental and societal institutions that emerge from the dialogue process. With this model, Volkan proposed that facilitators identify the group's underlying traumas to help all parties overcome resistances to dialogue and resolve their conflicts peacefully.

In this chapter, I build on Volkan's work, focusing my analysis on psychopolitical dialogues between delegates of opposing groups as pertains to the second phase of the Tree Model. I consider whether a group psychoanalytic approach comprising verbal expression and psychodrama could complement psycho-political dialogues, especially in the face of intractable deadlocks, so that the disputants can continue to work through the origins of their intractable conflicts. My intention is not to invalidate the political, socio-economic, cultural or religious factors that fuel conflicts or to challenge the efficacy of established mediation protocols but rather to expand the mediation tools that are currently in use. Peacemaking is a complex and dynamic process, often involving interactions with multiple interdependent actors and systems including national, regional and international actors with different agendas and interests. Decisions about the inclusion or exclusion of actors in the peacemaking process and the levels of authority and substitution of their representatives, as well as the flexibility, agility and innovation of the device, are necessary to manage uncertainty and achieve fruitful outcomes. The proposed device can thus be seen as part of a holistic and multidisciplinary approach to mediation and peacemaking, providing an additional perspective on complex dynamics and issues. No single theoretical or disciplinary approach can explain the nature of peacemaking and thus provides a unique framework to facilitate the process.

The proposed device is a found-and-created (Winnicott, 1965) framework that attempts to creatively rethink mediation practice in general and Volkan's model in particular. As Winnicott (1965) noted, a good object is not good unless it is created; however, the paradox is that the object must first be found in the environment to be subsequently created. Therefore, I do not propose a rigid setting with strict ground rules and techniques, which would run the risk of transforming the device into a fetish that hinders the analytical process and burdens the analytical relationship. The holding and containing functions of the frame depend not on ground rules, settings or techniques but on the unconscious ability to use another person's mind (Goldberg, 1989; Goldberg, as cited in Levine, 2009). The proposed device is to be understood as a malleable and re-created framework that can provide a comfortable envelope (Gabbard, 2007) and safeguard the 'analysing situation' (Donnet, 2001) that results from the patient's subjectivised use of the analytic setting. The 'analysing situation', as a structure that facilitates the ability to self-organise, disorganise and reorganise, can facilitate the mediation process.

A residential group psychoanalytic framework

Building on CEFFRAP's (Circles of French Studies for Training and Research: Psychoanalytic Approach to the Group, to Psychodrama, to the Institution) and Volkan's approaches, I would like to explore whether a residential group psychoanalytic framework can be extended to the field of mediation to complement peacemakers' strategies for working through the unconscious dynamics at play in dialogues.

Preliminary interviews with prospective participants would be conducted prior to the group psychoanalytic intervention. In the field of peacemaking, these interviews would need to include the representatives of the groups that will participate in the psycho-political dialogues. Such interviews eschew a diagnostic approach to understanding conflict and its effects in favour of a psychoanalytic stance of inquiry that generates potentially transformative insights. Prior diagnostic information would bias the psychoanalysts and create dissonance that impedes their ability to listen to unconscious dynamics. Getting to know participants and their groups through prior diagnosis, as in Volkan's first phase of the Tree Model, could bias psychoanalysts by creating preconceived notions about the conflict, its roots and the work required. It would be like working with families and groups with whom the psychoanalysts have relationships, which is inappropriate.

Thus, during the preliminary interviews, the psychoanalysts leading the group would assess the participants' readiness for the psychoanalytic group experience and sensitise them to the group psychoanalytic framework as a tool for facilitating and supporting transformative possibilities. The preliminary interviews provide an initial container that is safe enough for participants to begin to explore the roots of their difficulties and possibilities for change. These interviews are the first step towards change as they disrupt the dominant ways of doing things in the group and participants begin to explore the dominant storylines. Furthermore, the consultants are an integral part of the unfolding process, rather than neutral facilitators standing outside the system as in a diagnostic approach.

After the preliminary interviews, a psychoanalytic group would be set up. To ensure the fairness of the process, as in Volkan's model, the conflicting parties would be equally represented in the residential group. In addition, the delegates would have similar authority and influence. Participants would meet in the same place for a period of four days, two or three times a year over a period of several years. This would provide the group with a new experience that would unfold over time, fostering transformation.

Because this model is spread over a long period, the group would be semi-open, similar to Volkan's model, which would allow for flexibility. New participants would join the process as others left. New participants would be introduced to the modality of participation both in the preliminary interviews and in the act of forming the group. The decision to accept new participants would be taken by the two major groups represented in the psycho-political dialogues; the psychoanalysts would not be involved in this decision, as it would compromise their neutrality. The presence, absence and change of participants have an impact on the group and are an expression of its dynamics, which provides further material for analysis. Changes in participants could destabilise the group balance and block group processes; however, given the long lifespan of the group, these changes would allow for the emergence of group culture and eventually transformation (Gauthier, 1981, 1982). The absence and change of participants could also be a manifestation of the groups' experiences of separation, loss and mourning, or a provocation of such experiences (Talpin, 2011).

In concordance with CEFFRAP's model, participants would meet in four sessions per day of 75 minutes each. These would include small group sessions of 8–12 participants, which would be convened in parallel, and plenary sessions of verbal expression, where all participants and psychoanalysts would sit in a circle, face to face. Each small group would be led by two psychoanalysts rather than a multidisciplinary team, as is the case in Volkan's model (1999b, 2006). The psychoanalysts interpret the unconscious psychic dynamics of groups. Small group and individual dynamics are an integral part of the group process and an expression of the large groups' dynamics. Conflicts would not be analysed only when they get in the way (Volkan, 1999b, 2006).

The small group sessions would be of two types: back-to-back sessions and face-to-face groups. In back-to-back sessions, psychoanalysts and participants sit in a circle with their backs turned to the outside of the circle behind them. The suspension of the scopic function activates the auditory, olfactory and tactile senses (vibrations of the neighbour's skin). Attention is focused on speech, sounds, voice timbre and breath, giving rise to the 'back' and 'behind' of primitive anxieties and phantasies that are not usually triggered in the face-to-face framework (Kaës, 2015).

In face-to-face sessions, participants and psychoanalysts sit in a semicircle, which implicitly opens the space for psychodrama. Although psychoanalytic group psychodrama can be offered directly to participants without the preamble of the psychoanalytic verbal expression group, it is not usually indicated for groups that are overridden by enactments, such as when participants are at war with each other. In such cases, participants find it difficult to disengage from reality and access their phantasy world; they cannot play.

Volkan (1999b, 2006) noted that in political dialogues, a mini-conflict or disruptive situation sometimes breaks out at the beginning of the dialogue sessions. He saw this as a defence mechanism by which participants displace aggression onto an insignificant event to cope with the anxiety underlying the conflict. Mini-conflicts, in my view, are manifestations of central and lateral transference (probably perverse transference). The participants may be testing the psychoanalysts' holding ability, enacting within the group framework, the experience of the group and the link between its members so that they can be interpreted to gain insight. Furthermore, mini-conflicts can express the archaic facet of the *fraternal complex* (Kaës, 2008).

During psychoanalytic group work, the presenting problem is often the sole focus of the group's initial attention. Participants paradoxically want to maintain their current structure but demand change that will eliminate their problems. The problem is therefore the focus of common interest—to be used as a point of departure and return for further exploration between the parties. It contributes to the systemic balance of the group and expresses the inherent dynamics that must be addressed. Volkan (1999b, 2006) found that during the first two days of psycho-political dialogues, participants from opposing camps tend to focus on protecting their large group identity. On the third day, after facilitators have helped participants overcome their resistance, negotiations move forward. The fourth day usually focuses on practical proposals to reduce group tensions.

Therefore, to ensure transformation, psychoanalysts observe the dynamics and phenomena of the group. For example, like Volkan (1999b, 2006), they note and analyse the echo of external events on the group. Volkan (1999b, 2006) noted how participants from large opposing groups in psycho-political dialogues often experience a rapprochement, followed by a withdrawal, and later another rapprochement, and so on, like an accordion. He called this the accordion phenomenon. At the root of this phenomenon, according to Volkan, is the denial and acceptance of aggressive impulses towards the enemy group and attempts to protect large group identities. Through the accordion phenomenon, however, the group may be playing with new ways of connecting that were previously inaccessible. Through lateral transference, the group may be working through the paradoxical aspects of its relationships. The accordion phenomenon is an integral part of the group's experience and not just, as Volkan (1999b, 2006) stated, something to be allowed and tolerated so that the affective vacillation is replaced by more secure feelings that allow effective discussion. It is working through this expression of the link that would allow participants to gain insight and become a work group that, in my view, fulfils its primary task. This is only possible, in Volkan's (1999b, 2006) terms, in the space in between, where the accordion is neither too little nor too much squeezed.

In the model I propose, the suggestion of psychodrama can only come as a natural result of the psychoanalytic process of the group's verbal expression. As the group work progresses, the participants trust that the transitional space of the psychoanalytic field is safe. This allows them to explore the root causes of their conflicts. The transformation of the group can be seen in the emergence of dreams and playfulness among members, reflecting the ability to symbolise previously enacted anxieties and traumas. When participants trust the psychoanalytic space and feel safe enough, they become playful. They are better able to detach from reality, symbolise and access phantasy. In this way the psychoanalytic setting becomes a playground (Freud, 1914). It is in this atmosphere that psychoanalysts often propose psychodrama.

Volkan (1999b, 2006, 2011) noted that representatives of large groups often play and become playful during negotiations, especially when the situation is tense and dangerous. He found that describing the conflict in metaphorical terms can reduce the threat and lead participants to play with different ways of understanding their situation. This promotes empathy and addresses large group identity issues—which in turn contributes to successful negotiations. For example, during the Oslo Peace Process in 1992, Rifkind and Picco (2014) used role-playing, with Israelis representing the Palestinian position and vice versa, which helped lay the groundwork for the Camp David peace talks in 2000.

In his Tree Model, Volkan (1999b, 2006, 2011) created a space for participants to naturally become playful, which helps them transform their malignant relationships. The parties in conflict create effigies that represent their antagonists and their large group identities (Volkan, 2006, 2011). For example, Russian and Estonian negotiators used play as a way to reach an agreement, by being assigned the roles of rabbits and elephants. These animal effigies are, in my opinion, transitional objects (Winnicott, 1953, 1971), cathected with both narcissistic and object libidos. As first not-Me possessions, they imply the recognition of the other as not-Me, that is, the ability to accept differences and similarities. These plays reveal what is at stake for the group, its participants and their links. Volkan (1988, 1999b, 2006, 2013) noted that, while playing during psycho-political dialogues, participants manifest the accordion phenomenon.

Therefore, in the model I propose, psychodrama would not be imposed a priori, lest participants reject it or it trigger an explosive enactment of their traumatic experience that would not allow for interpretation and symbolisation. The role of the psychoanalysts would be to move the participants 'from a state of not being able to play into a state of being able to play' (Winnicott, 1971, p. 38).

The first day of group work would begin and end with a plenary session, with one face-to-face and one small back-to-back group session in between. For the remaining three days, each day would begin with small group sessions (face-to-face, back-to-back, then face-to-face) and end with a plenary session of verbal expression. Maintaining a fixed structure of plenaries and small groups, as CEFFRAP does, would provide a holding environment that promotes trust. Plenary sessions would not, as Volkan (1999b, 2006) argues, become less important and less frequent as the dialogue series progresses. Plenary sessions would play a role in revealing group dynamics and would be maintained.

In the framework I propose, and in line with the CEFFRAP model, the psychoanalytic group rules would apply to both the plenary and small group sessions. There is no requirement, as in Volkan's model (1999b, 2006), that the selected representatives of each of the small groups relate and summarise their experiences and perspectives of events. This would inflame envy and the *archaic fraternal complex* and produce perverse transferential and counter-transferential reactions. Moreover, to transform the life group into a psychoanalytic group and to define the boundaries between inside and outside, the rule of abstinence must be respected. Thus, in contrast to Volkan's model of psycho-political dialogues, the participants and the psychoanalysts leading the group would only interact during the sessions. Breaches of this rule by psychoanalysts and participants would be interpreted as enactments and expressions of perverse transference and *incestual* dynamics (Racamier, 1995), whereby the group and its constituent members maintain a confusion of boundaries between the Me and the not-Me and are dominated by primary process thinking and enactments. All material between sessions would be reintroduced during sessions, so that it would not remain unanalysed and negatively influence the group work.

When psychoanalysts come to psycho-political dialogue sessions, they suspend memory and desire (Bion, 1970). They focus on the group dynamics as they unfold in the here and now of the sessions, without trying to remember what happened in the preliminary interviews or in previous group sessions. Thus, in both plenary and small group sessions, as in the CEFFRAP model, psychoanalysts would observe, listen and interpret all group phenomena and effects, including transferences, as expressions of the psychic reality of the group as a whole and of its individual members and their intersubjective links. Although Volkan (1999b, 2006) notes the importance of the relationships between the facilitating team members for the success of psycho-political dialogues, his model does not examine and interpret inter-transference to shed light on the unconscious dynamics of the group, its participants and their links. In the model I propose, the group psychoanalysts are an integral part of the group psychoanalytic field. Thus, the role of the psychoanalysts would not be reduced to sharing their observations and working through any difficulties they might experience, as in Volkan's approach.

Final remarks

A psychoanalytically informed group approach could provide a complementary framework for conflict transformation in general and peacemaking dialogues in particular to detoxify contaminated relationships, promote dialogue and assist with overcoming impasses. This framework would provide a holding environment to help parties symbolise and transform their unconscious archaic anxieties and traumatic elements of their group history, rather than enacting them through violence and hostility.

With a group psychoanalytic framework of verbal expression and psychodrama, the mediation and peacemaking experience would be a process of reflection on the verbal, affective and behavioural material that unfolds so that the unconscious dynamics underlying conflicts could be interpreted and understood. Group psychoanalytically informed mediation would be a long-term process, as change can only be sustained if the group discovers it over time rather than having it imposed by a psychoanalyst. In this approach, psychoanalysts would accompany the conflicting groups in the direction of the desired change while respecting the rhythm of assimilation of the underlying dynamics of the conflict during this process of change. A psychoanalytic approach helps individuals and groups accept conflictuality as an inherent part of human nature, even in its most destructive manifestations. After all, human behaviour is the result of the interplay between two basic drives: Eros and Thanatos (Freud, 1920, 1930). A psychoanalytic approach seeks to 'widen the ego's perspective and enlarge its organisation, so that it can appropriate fresh portions of the id' (Freud, 1933, p. 80). Perhaps then, people could, as Freud (1933) argued, 'subordinate their instinctual life to the dictatorship of reason' (p. 213).

Finally, extending a psychoanalytic approach to work with representatives at the peace table is not enough to ensure the implementation of peace agreements. Despite their high level of authority and decision-making power, the progress of these representatives may not be in line with the psychology of the government or the groups they represent. This can create a divide that jeopardises the implementation and long-term success of peace treaties. This is the case regardless of the mediation protocol used. For the newly gained insights to ensure long-term social and political transformation, further psychological work is needed at the grassroots level, as Volkan noted in the third phase of his Tree Model. At this level, a group psychoanalytic device can complement the existing peacebuilding efforts.

References

Bion, W. R. (1970). *Attention and interpretation: A scientific approach to insight in psychoanalysis and groups.* London: Tavistock.

Donnet, J. (2001). From the fundamental rule to the analysing situation. *International Journal of Psychoanalysis, 82*: 129–140. https://doi.org/10.1516/0020757011600524

Freud, S. (1914). Remembering, repeating and working-through (further recommendations on the technique of psycho-analysis II). In: J. Strachey (Ed.), *The standard edition of the complete psychological works of Sigmund Freud, Volume XII (1911–1913): The case of schreber, papers on technique and other works* (pp. 145–156). London: The Hogarth Press.

Freud, S. (1920). Beyond the pleasure principle. In: J. Strachey (Ed.), *The standard edition of the complete psychological works of Sigmund Freud, Volume XVIII (1920–1922): Beyond the pleasure principle* (pp. 1–64). London: The Hogarth Press.

Freud, S. (1930). Civilization and its discontents. In: J. Strachey (Ed.), *The standard edition of the complete psychological works of Sigmund Freud, Volume XXI (1927–1931): The future of an illusion, civilization and its discontents and other works* (pp. 57–146). London: Hogarth Press.

Freud, S. (1933). New introductory lectures in psycho-analysis. In: J. Strachey (Ed.), *The standard edition of the complete psychological works of Sigmund Freud, Volume XXII (1932–1936): New introductory lectures in psycho-analysis and other works* (pp. 1–182). London: Hogarth Press.

Friedman, R. (2019). The 'group sandwich model' for international conflict using large groups as a societal developmental space. In: R. Friedman (Ed.), *Dream-telling, relations, and large groups* (pp 88–91). *New developments in group analysis.* The new international library of group analysis (Kindle edition). London & New York: Routledge.

Gabbard, G. (2007). Flexibility of the frame revisited. *Psychoanalytic Dialogues, 17*: 923–929. https://doi.org/10.1080/10481880701704100

Galtung, J. (2000). The transcend method at a glance: A one-page version. In: *Conflict transformation by peaceful means (The transcend method)—Participants'/trainers' manual.* United Nations. Retrieved from https://www.transcend.org/pctrcluj2004/TRANSCEND_manual.pdf.

Gauthier, M. (1981). Résistances caractéristiques à l'implantation de la «thérapie de groupe» dans un internat de rééducation pour délinquants [Characteristic resistances to the implementation of 'group therapy' in a re-education boarding school for delinquents]. *Revue Québécoise de Psychologie, 2*(2): 42–48.

Gauthier, M. (1982). La thérapie de groupe auprès de délinquants: Cinquante séances plus tard [Group therapy with offenders: Fifty sessions later]. *Revue Quebecoise de Psychologies, 3*(3): 30–47.

Goldberg, P. (1989). Actively seeking the holding environment—Conscious and unconscious elements in the building of a therapeutic framework. *Contemporary Psychoanalysis, 25*: 448–476. https://doi.org/10.1080/00107530.1989.10746312

Kaës, R. (2008). *Le Complexe Fraternel [The fraternal complex].* Paris: Dunod.

Kaës, R. (2015). *L'extension de la Psychanalyse: Pour une Métapsychologie de Troisième Type [The extension of psychoanalysis: For a metapsychology of the third type].* Paris: Dunod. https://doi.org/10.3917/dunod.kaes.2015.02

Lederach, J. P. (2014). *Little book of conflict transformation: Clear articulation of the guiding principles by a pioneer in the field.* New York, NY: Good Books.

Levine, A.R. (2009). Bending the frame and judgment calls in everyday practice. *Journal of American Psychoanalytic Association, 57*: 1209–1215. https://doi.org/10.1177/0003065109344339

Miall, H. (2004). *Conflict transformation: A multi-dimensional task.* Berlin: Berghof Research Center for Constructive Conflict Management. Retrieved from https://www.berghof-foundation.org/fileadmin/redaktion/Publications/Handbook/Articles/miall_handbook.pdf

Racamier, P. C. (1995). *L'inceste et l'incestuel [The incest and the incestual].* Paris: Éditions du Collège.

Rifkind, G., & Picco, G. (2014). *The fog of peace: The human face of conflict resolution.* London: I.B. Tauris & Co. https://doi.org/10.5040/9780755602957

Talpin, J. (2011). Le modèle du groupe dans l'analyse des pratiques: Groupe fermé/groupe ouvert, continuité/discontinuité dans l'institution [The group model in the analysis of practices: closed group/open group, continuity/discontinuity in the institution]. *Nouvelle Revue de Psychosociologie, 11*(1): 117–130. https://doi.org/10.3917/nrp.011.0117

Volkan, V. D. (1987). Psychological concepts useful in the building of political foundations between nations: Track II diplomacy. *Journal of the American Psychoanalytic Association, 35*: 903–935. https://doi.org/10.1177/000306518703500406

Volkan, V. D. (1988). *The need to have enemies and allies: From clinical practice to international relationships.* Northvale: Jason Aronson.

Volkan, V. D. (1999a). Psychoanalysis and diplomacy: Part III. Potentials for and obstacles against collaboration. *Journal of Applied Psychoanalytic Studies, 1*: 305–318. https://doi.org/10.1023/a:1023019619160

Volkan, V. D. (1999b). The Tree Model: A comprehensive psychological approach to unofficial diplomacy and the reduction of ethnic tension. *Mind and Human Interaction, 9*: 130–181.

Volkan, V. D. (2006). *Killing in the name of identity: A study of bloody conflicts.* Charlottesville, VA: Pitchstone Publishing.

Volkan, V. D. (2009). Large-group identity, international relations and psychoanalysis. *International Forum of Psychoanalysis, 18*(4): 206–213. https://doi.org/10.1080/08037060902727795

Volkan, V. D. (2011). Play and tract two diplomacy. In: M. C. Akhtar & M. Nayer (Eds.), *Play and playfulness: Developmental, clinical, and socio-cultural aspects* (pp. 150–71). New York, NY: Jason Aronson.

Volkan, V. D. (2013). Large-group-psychology in its own right: Large-group identity and peace-making. *International Journal of Applied Psychoanalytic Studies, 10*(3): 210–246. https://doi.org/10.1002/aps.1368

Volkan, V. D. (2014). *Psychoanalysis, international relations, and diplomacy.* London & New York: Routledge.

Winnicott, D. W. (1953). Transitional objects and transitional phenomena—A study of the first not-me possession. *The International Journal of Psychoanalysis, 34*: 89–97.

Winnicott, D. W. (1965). The maturational processes and the facilitating environment: Studies in the theory of emotional development. *The International Psychoanalytical Library, 64*: 1–276. London: The Hogarth Press and the Institute of Psychoanalysis.

Winnicott, D. W. (1971). *Playing and reality.* London: Tavistock Publications.

Chapter 9

A group psychoanalytic approach to the analysis of peacemakers' practices

Peacemakers deal with violent conflicts to reconcile adversaries and build peace. They often find themselves in crisis and precarious situations, exposed to stressors that affect their emotional well-being and influence their practice and the peacemaking process, both consciously and unconsciously. Horror and trauma are common, and peacemakers often find it difficult to maintain a space for psychic processing. As with other professionals in the social science and psychology fields, when peacemakers reach an impasse in their practice, this may be related to the difficulties of their working groups. Professionals and professional organisations suffer from the same pathologies they deal with (Bleger, 2003). Deep narcissistic wounds may be opened, accompanied by violent defences and enactments. Peacemakers may feel powerless, unable to cope, think, remember, act and even be. They may struggle with depression, sideration, physical symptoms and feelings of exhaustion and emptiness. They may lose their neutrality and attempt to manipulate, seduce and dominate the parties in conflict at the peace table to move the peace process forward, thereby denying the qualities of the parties and discrediting their perceptions, feelings and needs. Classical mediator training may not provide sufficient psychological tools to deal with such unconscious transferential and counter-transferential dynamics. An analysis of the practice tool can therefore help peacemakers to become aware of these dynamics to improve and develop their practice.

In this chapter, I propose to use a psychoanalytically oriented group framework to help peacemakers become aware of the unconscious dynamics underlying the professional aporias of their practice. This framework calls for peacemakers—working independently or under the umbrella of a specific institution on common or disparate conflicts—to elaborate on their professional practice, identity and identifications. The device I propose builds on the work of Circles of French Studies for Training and Research: Psychoanalytic Approach to the Group, to Psychodrama, to the Institution (CEFFRAP) to which I referred in Chapter 7.

In proposing the use of the above device, I do not mean to invalidate or question the effectiveness of established mediation training protocols, but

DOI: 10.4324/9781003545842-12

rather to offer a complementary method of inquiry (Bion, 1965; Ogden, 2007). This tool would allow peacemakers to look at their professional practice from a different perspective. It might help them to better understand the difficult situations they often face, to cope with the challenges of their professional practice and to be better able to facilitate transformation. In addition, as few previous studies have explored the role of group psychoanalytic methods in analysing mediation practices, the approach of this chapter may stimulate further research. The tool can also be applied beyond peacemaking practices to include, for example, mediation practices related to climate change conflicts or refugee resettlement.

Before elaborating on the proposed framework, I would like to reflect on trauma and trauma work, which often underlie the dynamics of peacemaking and influence the practice of peacemakers and the peacemaking process.

Trauma and trauma work

Violent conflicts and wars are traumatic. They are painful and distressing events for which people are unprepared, and they disrupt psychic functioning. They provoke an excess of arousal that breaches the individual's capacity for containment (or arousal shield). In addition, these conflicts threaten one's ability to think, distort one's sense of time and trigger the compulsion to repeat. As a result, traumatised individuals feel helpless and alienated from themselves and others, and feel split and amputated from part of their ego, with a diminished sense of self (Bokanowski, 2002). Intense narcissistic rage is often a protection from the painful feelings of vulnerability.

Traumatised individuals deny the unbearable affect and the traumatic event, if not entire parts of reality (Rosenblum, 2009). They encapsulate their experience in autistic chambers (Hopper & Weinberg, 2018), dead psychic zones or crypts, without representation or symbolisation (Abraham & Torok, 1984). Encapsulation can either encapsulate the traumatic experience or shield the healthy parts of the self from that experience (Hopper & Weinberg, 2018). In the latter positive version, the traumatised individual withdraws into psychic retreats (Steiner, 1993). These psychic retreats are hiding places that provide an alternative shelter from relationships and reality. They protect the individual from archaic fears and unbearable guilt and, perversely, offer narcissistic and masochistic gratifications. However, despite their benefits, psychic retreats paradoxically trap the vital parts of the self and endanger contact with reality and others. Moreover, the non-representable and non-symbolised traumatic elements can become radioactive. These elements enter the psychic apparatus of others without them having control over their entry, implantation and effects (Gampel, 1993, 1998).

Trauma work is therefore necessary to *counter* the negative and destructive effects of trauma. However, psychoanalysts working with traumatised clients may become vicariously traumatised (Pearlman & Saakvitne, 1995) through their empathic engagement with their clients. Traumatised clients may defensively use projective identification to detoxify their experiences of their pathogens. In doing so, they attempt to rid themselves of unwanted impulses and intolerable affects. They also attempt—out of primitive envy and the desire to cling parasitically to others as a valued object—to dominate, devalue and control them (Horwitz, 1983). Thus, in a psychoanalytic setting, traumatised clients may manipulate the framework and discredit the psychoanalyst and the psychoanalytic process through envious transference. The psychoanalytic field thus becomes perverse, characterised by paradoxicality, mystification and ambiguity. By projecting onto the outside world, the envious attempt to understand, master and change their world (Hopper, 2003). Psychoanalysts risk internalising and identifying with the unconscious, radioactive remnants of their clients' memories of social violence. Through this radioactive identification (Gampel, 1998), they risk becoming crypt carriers (Torok, 1968) of intolerable affects and denied and incorporated lost objects.

Confrontation with the unrepresentable leads to negative therapeutic reactions marked by passivation and the logic of despair (Green, as cited in Di Rocco, 2017)—in other words, feelings of helplessness and the experience of the impossibility of initiating change. As a result, the psychoanalysts' practices, identities and identifications may suffer. Their frames of reference, worldviews and ego capacities are transformed, mimicking the symptoms of their clients. Psychoanalysts may lose the ability to distinguish psychic reality from physical reality, phantasy from events and the internal from the external. Janin (2014) refers to this trauma effect as a topical collapse. Forced to 'lend themselves to unbinding' (Gaillard, as cited in Pinel & Gaillard, 2020, p. 305), these professionals often search for spaces to think. Exploring their roles and experiences—as well as their counter-transference and vicarious traumatisation—can inform their interventions, enrich their work and protect them and their clients (Pearlman & Saakvitne, 1995).

At the peace table, peacemakers must deal with the violence inherent in the belligerent situations that motivate their encounters as peacemakers. Volkan (1987, 2013) noted how such advocates must deal with the present traumas of large groups, their past traumas, their transgenerational transmission and the need to do the work of mourning. However, despite being a pioneer in moving from behind the couch to the peace table, Volkan did not explore how peacemakers and back-channel mediators are confronted with archaic and unrepresentable psychic phenomena and how they may subsequently become vicariously traumatised and contaminated by the radioactive traumatic elements of the violence they are dealing with.

In addition, there is a paucity of literature on the analysis of counter-transference processes to understand the impact of the social unconscious on group work or peace talks. There is also a lack of literature on the study of counter-transference dynamics during peace talks. For example, Volkan analysed peace talks and back-channel mediation dynamics as an outside observer rather than as part of the mediation field and its transference processes. He (2004) highlighted his prejudices and feelings when dealing with key participants in peace talks. He noted the need for personal work to maintain neutrality. However, he did not analyse the participants' prejudices and feelings as counter-transferential reactions that can provide insight into group dynamics, inform their interventions and enhance their work. Although counter-transference processes are defensive phenomena, they are also tools for understanding unconscious dynamics.

At the peace table, the memory lapses, disinterest and detachment of the peacemaker, or their attempts to neutralise their affects and suppress their prejudices may point to black holes, social-psychic retreats or what I would call social crypts of the groups represented there. These social crypts reflect their encapsulation defences and the psychic transmission or contagion of trauma that must be worked through. In addition, the peacemaker's feelings of incapacity, sideration and melancholy may indicate the defences against mass melancholia and the inability of the groups (represented at the peace table) to do the work of mourning (Mitscherlich & Mitscherlich, 1975).

Thus, a psychoanalytically informed group approach to practice analysis could provide a complementary framework to help peacemakers decontaminate themselves from the radioactive effect of the potentially traumatic elements of their profession, combat melancholisation processes (Di Rocco, 2017) and protect them from becoming crypt carriers of unbearable affects. It would help them to mourn their professional ideal and triumphant narcissism, and to work through their disappointments and sufferings to transform their practice. It would also provide peacemakers with complementary experiential learning and training to develop their practice, especially since reflecting on practice is a work of theorisation that is not limited to the presentation of group experiences.

The clinical framework of practice analysis

Analysis of practice as a training approach has been developing since the 1940s. It was initiated by the psychoanalyst Michael Balint to improve the relational practice of doctors. The professional relationship is at the centre of the analysis. The Balint group invites participants with the same functions to associate freely regarding their professional practice to explore their counter-transference dynamics, unconscious affects and phantasies which, if neither understood nor accepted, could undermine professional competence (Blanchard-Laville & Fablet, 1998). It is an applied psychoanalysis that goes beyond the boundaries of the classical cure or medical consultation (Laplanche, as cited in Henri-Ménassé, 2009). Practice analysis was also inspired by the work of French psychoanalysts such as René Kaës and Didier Anzieu (Henri-Ménassé, 2009). Subsequently, the health, social and special education sectors integrated this analysis of professional practice, most often from a group psychoanalytic perspective (Gadeau, 2004).

A psychoanalytically oriented practice analysis provides a space for sharing, exchanging and listening to each other and is most often used by professionals with a predominantly relational component, such as doctors, teachers or social workers. It allows participants to distance themselves from lived situations and reflect on professional experiences by sharing them in the group (Henri-Ménassé, 2009). In this sense, psychoanalytically oriented practice analysis is similar to a psychoanalytic training approach, which implies supervision, that is, a super-vision or a superior view.

Psychoanalytically informed practice analysis is often called upon to support professionals who find themselves blocked in relationships where symbolisation processes are at risk (Henri-Ménassé, 2009). It offers them a time to talk about their practice freely and confidentially. This approach to practice analysis helps them to reflect on non-mentalised elements and repeated enactments at an individual and collective level. It also helps them to explore the link with the other and with the institution. If these links are a source of suffering, are characterised by defensiveness or are questioning of self and others, they can disorient professional practice. Practice analysis, like all analysis, is therefore a dynamic attempt to unbind and reorganise established links between things, objects, affects and their representations (Henri-Ménassé, 2009).

To facilitate engaging in psychic development work and accessing the archaic layers of a group's psychic apparatus, a psychoanalytically oriented practice analysis is conducted in regular, small group sessions of a fixed duration and rhythm. Regularity and duration provide a sense of security. They promote the progressive de-condensations of entangled projections and foster the processing of unbearable affects and anxiety-provoking representations (Henri-Ménassé, 2009). This is important when professional practices continually generate the unthinkable and mobilise defences. Moreover, during these sessions, the psychoanalyst listens with benevolent neutrality. They renounce the position of model, teacher or advisor—the subject presumed to know—as can be the case in other process group frameworks. Instead, they focus on the development of the group's unconscious functioning. They guide the group in identifying the object of reflection, which is not defined in advance. A participant evokes a primary situation and the reflection is organised around elements that have sufficient resonance among the other group participants.

The associations made by the participants in relation to the professional experiences recounted clarify the transferential dynamics between the persons recounting the situation and those about whom they speak. This associative thread also allows the group participants to reflect—in their own way and at their own pace—on their own counter-transferential positions and their different representations of their professional practices, professional identities and identifications. The group process helps the participants work through and reappropriate unbearable affects and archaic anxieties. This helps the participants reinvest in thinking and listening to others and supports their initial choice of professional identity.

Thus, practice analysis groups, like Balint groups, are process groups (Swiller, 2011). This does not mean that there are no therapeutic effects (Blanchard-Laville & Fablet, 1998; Henri-Ménassé, 2009; Swiller, 2011). However, unlike the Balint approach, the practice analysis group approach is registered at the institutional level; that is, it is aimed at groups belonging to the same structure or training (Henri-Ménassé, 2009). Its main objective is to support or relaunch the work of intersubjectivity, to promote team bonds and the ability of each individual and the whole to invest their part in the fulfilment of the primary institutional task. Furthermore, in a practice analysis framework, unlike the Balint technique, the psychoanalyst does not focus on the reporter of the case, but on the case shared by the group. Focusing on the exposed case rather than the exponent attenuates defensive movements and persecutory anxieties. The reporter's singular object becomes a group object, triggering identification and de-identification movements in group members (Gadeau, 2004).

The psychoanalyst in a practice analysis group inspired by the CEFFRAP model, unlike the psychoanalyst in a Balint group, observes the psychic reality of the group as a whole, the individual members and their intersubjective links (Kaës, 2014, 2016). As I highlighted in Chapter 7, they listen to the associative chain and phantasmatic resonance of the group. They do not only focus on the transferential dynamics at play between the practitioner and their client, but also interpret all transferential group dynamics (Kaës, 2010). They interpret all group dynamics as an echo of the dynamics of the case under analysis.

Usually, group psychoanalytically oriented practice analyses, like Balint groups, are conducted only in face-to-face verbal sessions. However, the CEFFRAP model incorporates group psychodrama into its device (Kaës et al., 2003), as play allows access to the most archaic levels of the psyche, which are usually held in the body and may not be accessible through verbal forms of expression.

To set up a psychoanalytically oriented practice analysis group and begin the psychoanalytic work, the psychoanalyst leading the group announces the psychoanalytic framework. The practice analysis group provides a holding environment (Winnicott, 1960) and acts as an excitation barrier. It becomes a group psychic apparatus (Kaës, 2000) that transforms the psychic reality and detoxifies the traumatic experiences of the group as a whole, its participants and their intersubjective links.

A group psychoanalytic framework for analysing peacemakers' practices

Given the nature of peacemaking work, which often involves metaphorically navigating through explosive minefields, and inspired by CEFFRAP's psychoanalytically oriented group device, I propose a composite psychoanalytic framework of face-to-face verbal expression sessions and group psychodrama to more effectively uncover and transform the unconscious archaic anxieties and dynamics that often plague peacemakers and influence their practices. In this framework, however, psychodrama would not be imposed without the preamble of group psychoanalytic verbal expression. The reason for this is that peacemakers may be affected by the radioactive effects of the content of their profession and may find it difficult to disengage from reality and access their phantasy world. In other words, they cannot play. As I argued in Chapter 8, psychodrama can only come as a natural result of the psychoanalytic process.

Thus, to encourage and support the possibility of professional transformation, the psychoanalyst leading the group would conduct preliminary interviews to explore the participants' requests, assess their readiness for the psychoanalytic group experience and sensitise them to it. In their request for practice analysis, participants paradoxically seek change that will resolve their problems, while at the same time they wish to remain attached to their complaint and preserve their current structure. Their paradoxical position reflects narcissistic dynamics, archaic superegos and ideals, and oscillations between feelings of impotence and omnipotence (Kaës et al., 2003). The participants want to reflect on the unbearable elements they are repeatedly confronted with in the relational aspects of their profession. They also want to regain their ability to think.

However, their demand for immobility helps them to avoid unspoken suffering (Henri-Ménassé, 2009). By working through their paradoxical position in a practice analysis group, peacemakers can gain insight into their own professional archaic functioning and ideals. In addition, through counter-transferential analysis, they can gain insight into the archaic functioning and ideals of the groups represented at the peace table. During these preliminary interviews, the psychoanalyst would inform the prospective participants about the structure of group practice analysis and the possibility of using psychodrama as a tool for further exploration. This would build trust and avoid stirring up resistance.

In sessions, participants would sit in a semicircle rather than in a circle as in the verbal expression process groups. This spatial structure would metaphorically open the space for participants to move from a closed, circular and blocked professional situation to an open one where there is another way of being and doing. It would also implicitly open the space for psychodrama by demarcating the space where the participants and the psychoanalyst sit and verbally associate freely from an empty space in front of them (where the role-playing takes place). Thus, the temporal structure would potentially include time for verbal expression and elaboration of a play theme, role-playing and reflecting on the role-playing experience. Body language can be heard as one of the possible languages of the social unconscious and the repetition of the trauma, like a bodily act. The social unconscious is expressed in non-verbal communication (Klimova, 2018; Wotton, 2018). Thus, through this bodily work, participants can become aware of, symbolise and transform the non-representable remnants of the radioactive influences of the external world within them (Gampel, 1993).

Final remarks

In this chapter, I have proposed extending the group psychoanalytic framework to the field of peacemaking. As a method of inquiry, the proposed framework offers a psychoanalytic experience that should not be reduced to an invariant technique or procedure (Bion, 1965; Ogden, 2007). Thus, further research must test the effectiveness of the proposed tool in developing peacemaking practices and, if necessary, adapt it to this field of work so that this found-and-created framework (Winnicott, 1965) can be efficacy in fulfilling its primary task. The direct application of a group model to peacemaking practices, without a close analysis of the complex psychic movements specific to these practices to adapt it, can—as Kaës (2015) argues in *L'Extension de la Psychanalyse* (The Extension of Psychoanalysis)—be a reductive and simplistic form of applied psychoanalysis that paralyses thinking and hinders the work of intersubjectivity and trans-subjectivity.

References

Abraham, N., & Torok, M. (1984). 'The lost object—me': Notes on identification within the crypt. *Psychoanalytic Inquiry, 4*: 221–242. https://doi.org/10.1080/07351698409533542

Bion, W. R. (1965). *Transformations: Change from learning to growth* (Vol. 5, pp. 1–172). London: Tavistock.

Blanchard-Laville, C., & Fablet, D. (1998). *L'Analyse des Pratiques Professionnelles (l') Nouvelle e (Savoir et Formation) [The analysis of professional practices (the) new e (Knowledge and training)]* (Kindle edition). Paris: L'Harmattan.

Bleger, J. (2003). Le groupe comme institution et le groupe dans les institutions [The group as an institution and the group in institutions]. In: R. Kaes, J. Bleger, E. Enriquez, F. Fonrari, P. Fustier, R. Roussillon, & J. P. Vidal. (Eds.), *L'Institution et les institutions [The institution and the institutions]* (pp. 47–61). Paris: Dunod.

Bokanowski, T. (2002). Traumatisme, traumatique, trauma. *Revue Française de Psychanalyse, 66*: 745–757. https://doi. org/10.3917/rfp.663.0745

Di Rocco, V. (2017). Espoir et désespoir... dans les groups d'analyse de la pratique [Hope and despair in groups for analysing practices]. *Revue de Psychothérapie Psychanalytique de Groupe, 68*: 81–88. https://doi.org/10.3917/rppg.068.0081

Gadeau, L. (2004). Cadre et technique dans l'analyse des pratiques professionnelles à orientation psychanalytique [Framework and technique in the analysis of professional practices with a psychoanalytic orientation]. *Psychologues et Psychologies, 176*: 4–6.

Gampel, Y. (1993). Access to the non-verbal through modelling in the psychoanalytic situation. *British Journal of Psychotherapy, 9*(3): 280–290. https://doi.org/10.1111/j.1752-0118.1993.tb01227.x

Gampel, Y. (1998). Reflections on countertransference in psychoanalytic work with child survivors of the Shoah. *The Journal of the American Academy of Psychoanalysis and Dynamic Psychiatry, 26*: 343–368. https://doi.org/10.1521/ jaap.1.1998.26.3.343

Henri-Ménassé, C. (2009). *Analyse de la Pratique en Institution: Scène, Jeux, En-jeux [Analysis of practice in an institution: Scene, play, issues]* (Kindle edition). Toulouse: Erès.

Hopper, E. (2003). *The social unconscious: Selected papers (International library of group analysis book 22)* (Kindle edition). Philadelphia, PA: Jessica Kingsley Publishers.

Hopper, E., & Weinberg, H. (2018). *The social unconscious in persons, groups and societies: Mainly theory.* The new international library of group analysis book (Kindle edition., Vol. 1). London & New York: Routledge.

Horwitz, L. (1983). Projective identification in dyads and groups. *International Journal of Group Psychotherapy, 33*(3): 259–279.

Janin, C. (2014). Corps étrangers: Entre monde interne et réalité matérielle [Foreign bodies: Between internal world and material reality]. *Revue Française de Psychanalyse, 78*: 1544–1550. https://doi.org/10.3917/rfp.785.1544

Kaës, R. (2000). *L'appareil Psychique Groupal [The group psychic apparatus].* Paris: Dunod.

Kaës, R. (2010). *La Parole et le Lien: Associativité et le Travail Psychique dans les Groups [The speech and the link: Associativity and psychic work in groups].* Paris: Dunod.

Kaës, R. (2014). Métapsychologie des espaces psychiques coordonnés [Metapsychology of coordinated psychic spaces]. *Revue de Psychothérapie Psychanalytique de Groupe, 62*: 7–23. https://doi.org/10.3917/rppg.062.0007

Kaës, R. (2016). Link and transference within three interfering psychic spaces. *Couple and Family Psychoanalysis, 6*: 181–193.

Kaës, R. (2015). *L'extension de la psychanalyse: Pour une métapsychologie de troisième type [The extension of psychoanalysis: For a metapsychology of the third type].* Dunod. https://doi.org/10.3917/dunod.kaes.2015.02

Kaës, R., Missenard, A., Nicolle, O., Benchimol, M., Blanchard, A.-M., Claquin, M., & Villier, J. (2003). *Le Psychodrame Psychanalytique de Groupe [Group psychoanalytic psychodrama].* Paris: Dunod.

Klimova, H. (2018). The unbearable appeal of totalitarianism and the collective self: An inquiry into the social nature of non-verbal communication. In: E. Hopper & H. Weinberg (Eds.), *The social unconscious in persons, groups and societies: The foundation matrix extended and reconfigured.* The new international library of group analysis book 3 (Kindle edition., pp. 89–105). London & New York: Routledge.

Mitscherlich, A., & Mitscherlich, M. (1975). *The inability to mourn: Principles of collective behavior.* New York, NY: Grove Press.

Ogden, T. H. (2007). Elements of analytic style: Bion's clinical seminars. *The International Journal of Psychoanalysis, 88*(5): 1185–1200. https://doi.org/10.1516/ijpa.2007.1185

Pearlman, L. A., & Saakvitne, K. W. (1995). *Trauma and the therapist: Counter-transference and vicarious traumatization in psychotherapy with incest survivors.* New York, NY: W.W. Norton & Co.

Pinel, J. P., & Gaillard, G. (2020). *Le Travail Psychanalytique en Institution: Manuel de Cliniques Institutionnelles [Psychoanalytic work in institutions: Manual of institutional clinics]* (Kindle edition). Paris: Dunod.

Rosenblum, R. (2009). Postponing trauma: The dangers of telling. *The International Journal of Psychoanalysis*, 90(6), 1319–1340.

Steiner, J. (1993). *Psychic retreats: Pathological organizations in psychotic, neurotic and borderline patients.* London & New York: Routledge.

Swiller, H. I. (2011). Process groups. *International Journal of Group Psychotherapy*, 61(2): 262–273. https://doi.org/10.1521/ ijgp.2011.61.2.262

Torok, M. (1968). Maladie du deuil et phantasme du cadavre exquis [The illness of mourning and the phantasy of the exquisite corpse]. *Revue Française de Psychanalyse*, 32: 715–733.

Volkan, V. D. (1987). Psychological concepts useful in the building of political foundations between nations: Track II diplomacy. *Journal of the American Psychoanalytic Association*, 35: 903–935. https://doi.org/10.1177/000306518703500406

Volkan, V. D. (2004). *Blind trust: Large groups and their leaders in times of crisis and terror.* Charlottesville, VA: Pitchstone Publishing.

Volkan, V. D. (2013). Large-group-psychology in its own right: Large-group identity and peace-making. *International Journal of Applied Psychoanalytic Studies*, 10(3): 210–246. https://doi.org/10.1002/aps.1368

Winnicott, D. W. (1960). The theory of the parent–infant relationship. *International Journal of Psychoanalysis*, 41: 585–595.

Winnicott, D. W. (1965). The maturational processes and the facilitating environment: Studies in the theory of emotional development. *The International Psychoanalytical Library*, 64:1–276. London: The Hogarth Press and the Institute of Psychoanalysis.

Wotton, L. (2018). The musical foundation matrix: Communicative musicality as a mechanism for the transmission and elaboration of co-created unconscious social processes. In: E. Hopper & H. Weinberg (Eds.), *The social unconscious in persons, groups and societies: The foundation matrix extended and reconfigured.* The new international library of group analysis book 3 (Kindle edition., pp. 107–126). London & New York: Routledge.

Chapter 10

A group psychoanalytic *social dreaming matrix* for peacemakers and peacebuilders

In Chapters 8 and 9, I proposed a group psychoanalytic device to help peacemakers decontaminate themselves and their practice from vicarious trauma, and to provide them with a complementary tool to use at the peace table in their efforts to promote transformation. In this chapter, I will elaborate on a group psychoanalytic *social dreaming matrix* as another complementary device for peacemakers and peacebuilders.

A brief overview of the *social dreaming matrix*

In 1982, Gordon Lawrence proposed the *social dreaming matrix* as a non-psychoanalytic tool for elaborating group processes, especially those related to shared political and cultural realities (Manley, 2014; Noack, 2010). Since then, the *social dreaming matrix* has been used in a variety of social and organisational contexts. The *social dreaming matrix* provides an intersubjective space where people share their night-time dreams to access the social unconscious and discover new thoughts through free association and amplification (Lawrence, 1998, as cited in Hopper & Weinberg, 2018). For Lawrence (as cited in Noack, 2010), dreams are the 'imaginative replay of our state of being in our social world and a rehearsal of how we are to become in relation to our environment' (p. 674). Dreaming transforms mentally indigestible traumatic experiences into dreams that aid thinking (Bion, 1984). Dreams are the royal road not only to the dreamer's inner world, as Freud argued, but also to their environmental difficulties (Friedman, 2019). Dreaming and dream-telling are successive and complementary stages of the emotional digestion process, both for the dreamer and for members of their social environment. 'Dream-telling is the re-dreaming of the dream through the other' (Friedman, 2019, p. 29).

The *social dreaming matrix has* its roots in psychoanalysis and group studies (Manley, 2014). However, in contrast to Tavistock's approach to groups, Lawrence saw dreams as important group material that should not be confined to individual psychoanalysis. He also emphasised the creative side of the unconscious that can facilitate change, rather than its defensive side or the need to make it conscious to facilitate the primary task of the group.

DOI: 10.4324/9781003545842-13

While individual and group therapeutic dream interventions focus on the Oedipal, *social dreaming* examines them from the perspective of the Sphinx, focusing on the unconscious thoughts and knowledge contained in the dream narrative rather than the dreamer's psyche (Hopper & Weinberg, 2018). For Bion (1961, 1963), the Sphinx generates curiosity through its enigma and represents a method of knowledge. As a non-psychoanalytic method, the *social dreaming matrix* bypasses resistance to the unknown and promotes new thoughts and insights that transcend the subjective focus of individual psychotherapy and the group-centred focus of Group Relations events (Lawrence, as cited in Manley, 2014).

To differentiate the *social dreaming matrix* from Group Relations Conferences, Lawrence provided the *social dreaming matrix* with a specific denomination, framework and primary task. Despite these new parameters, Lawrence (1998) understood that group dynamics persisted in the Matrix but did not focus on them. He perceived *social dreaming* and group dynamics as the two lenses of a binocular informing the Matrix; however, to access the *social unconscious*, he advocated a non-psychoanalytic monocular vision of the Matrix emphasising *social dreaming*. He did not look psychoanalytically through the group dynamics lens to access the social unconscious. Looking psychoanalytically through two lenses of *social dreaming* and group dynamics provides a wider perspective of the social unconscious, generating knowledge.

I argue that the *social dreaming matrix*, from a psychoanalytic perspective, is a group whose primary task is sharing nocturnal dreams and associations freely to generate insight into the social unconscious. Both group material and transferential dynamics provide additional knowledge and transform thinking. In addition, similar to a group psychoanalytic psychodrama, whose primary task is role-playing, I see the *social dreaming* matrix and subsequent *dream reflection dialogue* as two moments of a group whose primary task is *social dreaming*. This group psychoanalytic binocular vision approach is a found-and-created (Winnicott, 1965) device that rediscovers and recreates the non-psychoanalytic object-*social dreaming matrix* framework proposed by Lawrence.

To support my thesis, I draw on the work of Circles of French Studies for Training and Research: Psychoanalytic Approach to the Group, to Psychodrama, to the Institution (CEFFRAP). Unlike the Tavistock Group Relation Conferences, CEFFRAP listened not only to the overall psychic reality of the group but also to its individual members and their intersubjective links. Moreover, unlike the Tavistock Group Relation Conferences, CEFFRAP did not dismiss the importance of dreams within groups. On the contrary, as highlighted in Chapter 7, the group has a common and shared oneiric space in which there is polyphony of dreaming, that is, interwoven dream processes and images that both reveal and influence the dynamics of the group as a whole, its members and their links (Kaës, 2002). Kaës perceives the dreamer as both the subject of their own unconscious and a *dream carrier* for the group. Thus, when a group member shares a dream, the group is *dreaming collectively*. However, CEFFRAP did not propose, as Lawrence did, a group whose primary task is *social dreaming*, nor did it frame dreams as expressions of the social unconscious. Instead, as highlighted in Chapter 7, it saw the group as endowed with its own psychic apparatus (Kaës, 2000) and interpreted dreams as imaginary accomplishments of the group's repressed libidinal and aggressive drives.

I would like to extend CEFFRAP's approach to the *social dreaming matrix* to complement its primary task of providing additional insight into the social unconscious as well as external socio-political and cultural realities. The group is a projective surface for culture and society (Anzieu, 1984). Society as a very large group is defined not only by its socio-economic, cultural and political structures (the foundation matrix), but also by its repressed libidinal and death drives (Fromm, as cited in Hopper & Weinberg, 2018). These drives, coupled with repressed and split-off elements of external reality and its internal representations, as well as collective anxieties, defences, phantasies, myths and memories, constitute the social unconscious core, that is, its relational and communicational dynamic matrix (Hopper & Weinberg, 2018). Consequently, a *social dreaming matrix*, which psychoanalytically interprets dreams as the imaginary realisation of the repressed drives of the Matrix as a whole, its members and their links, can provide insights into the foundation (the sociocultural historical setting) and dynamic matrices of the *social unconscious*. In addition, I propose that CEFFRAP's group psychoanalytic psychodrama elaboration can clarify the temporal and spatial configurations of the *social dreaming matrix* and the dream-reflection dialogue framework.

To elucidate, I elaborate on the *social dreaming matrix* and *dream reflection dialogue* frameworks from a group psychoanalytic perspective.

The social dreaming matrix's framework

To launch a *social dreaming matrix,* the hosts define the framework of the Matrix. From a group psychoanalytic perspective (Kaës, 2015), this entails a paternal function that defines the working laws of the Matrix and acts as an excitation barrier conducive to symbolisation and transformation. It also entails a maternal function that contains, shapes and transforms the psychic reality of the Matrix as a whole, its members and their links. However, in denominating *social dreaming* a Matrix, from the Latin word for uterus (a mental receptacle of creativity), Lawrence emphasised the maternal function of the framework at the expense of its paternal function.

From a group psychoanalytic perspective, the Matrix's framework distinguishes the *social dreaming matrix* from the life group by establishing the *here and now* of the Matrix and the *there and then* of group life. The session structure establishes a new, different world with its own specific boundaries, rules, founders and psychic functioning, creating a dynamic new field

(Baranger & Baranger, 2008), a *transitional space* (Winnicott, 1953) where the self meets the other, reality meets fantasy and dreams become *transitional objects* (Manley, 2010).

The Matrix is endowed with a psychic apparatus that transforms the psychic reality of the Matrix as a whole, its participants and their links. Lawrence (as cited in Baglioni & Fubini, 2013) referred to intersubjective links when he argued that the Matrix, as a process, embodies the emotional and thinking web in social relationships, which are usually unacknowledged and unaddressed. Thus, contrary to Lawrence's argument that the shared dream no longer belongs to the dreamer once voiced in the Matrix, the dream (from a group psychoanalytic perspective) is an expression not only of the Matrix as a whole but also of its members and their links. As transitional objects, dreams are possessions of both Me and not-Me (Winnicott, 1953). Furthermore, by understanding the personal and social aspects of dream-telling, the relationship between self and culture is transformed (Manley, 2010).

The rules of the *social dreaming matrix* define the spatio-temporal setting, the role of the hosts and the modalities of sharing to reveal the social unconscious.

The temporal setting

The temporal structure of the Matrix is often divided into two moments: the *social dreaming* matrix, a time for freely sharing nocturnal dreams and associations to expand the dream narrative, and *dream reflection dialogue*, for elaborating on the *social dreaming matrix* experience. This temporal configuration is reminiscent of three moments in the temporal structure of group psychoanalytic psychodrama: free association to imagine a play theme, role-playing and elaboration of the role-playing experience.

The spatial setting

In the *social dreaming matrix*, chairs are arranged in a beehive or snowflake pattern (Figure 10.1), with participants sitting at different angles to the centre.

With this spatial modification, Lawrence (as cited in Manley, 2014) aimed to discourage face-to-face engagement between participants and hierarchical distinctions between hosts and participants, which he thought would reduce group dynamics and facilitate dream sharing. He thought that group dynamics would be reduced when participants did not look at each other. The dream, as group material, belongs to the Matrix, not the dreamer; and since the dream reveals our state of being and our relationship to our social world, attention focuses on the dream's sociopolitical dynamics and realities, not the dreamer's individual intrapsychic conflicts.

However, despite this spatial configuration, intimacy is generated. Telling a dream is an intimate act (Friedman, 2019). Participants continue relating

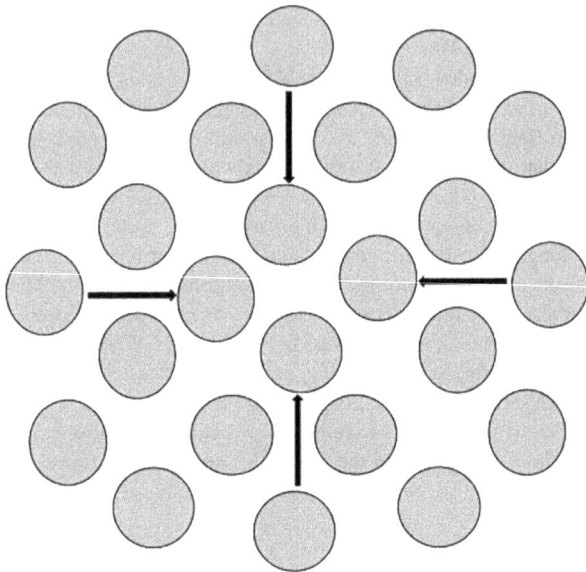

Figure 10.1 Arrangement of chairs in the *social dreaming matrix*.

to each other, and group dynamics are elicited (although Lawrence did not address them). As with back-to-back group psychoanalytic sessions where psychoanalysts and participants sit in a circle looking outwards, the seating configuration of the Matrix reduces or suspends the scopic function and re-focuses attention on speech, sound, voice timbre and breath, which generates archaic anxieties and phantasies of the *back and behind* (Kaës, 2015). Listening to the transferential dynamics triggered by the spatial configuration of the Matrix can reduce resistance and facilitate the Matrix's primary task.

In addition, to demarcate the second moment of the Matrix, the *dream reflection dialogue* participants sit in a circle. The spatial configurations of the *social dreaming matrix* and the *dream reflection dialogue* are reminiscent of the spatial structure of a semicircular group psychoanalytic psychodrama to outline spaces for verbal expression and role play (Kaës et al., 2003).

The hosts' role

The hosts of the *social dreaming matrix* announce the framework of the Matrix, manage the Matrix and help to focus on the primary task of the Matrix. In defining and guaranteeing the framework, there is an asymmetry

(Kaës et al., 2003) and a hierarchical distinction between hosts and participants which, contrary to Lawrence's assumption, is not erased by the seating arrangement. This asymmetry produces transference, which, when analysed, produces insight. However, the Matrix hosts do not address transference and assume that the spatial configuration reduces (if not eliminates) it.

In addition, similar to group psychoanalysts, hosts encourage regular presence, confidentiality and free association. However, the hosts of the *social dreaming matrix* do not incorporate the rule of abstinence into the framework. They share their dreams during the Matrix and interact with participants outside it. Since the rule of abstinence demarcates the boundaries between the Matrix and life spaces, the violation of this rule is, for psychoanalysts, a perverse enactment that blurs these boundaries and the symbolic nature of the transitional space, as happens with individual psychoanalytic work. If analysed, this breach can illuminate the underlying group dynamics unfolding in the Matrix and protect the primary task of Matrix from their potentially negative effects. Furthermore, unlike group psychoanalysts, the hosts do not interpret violations of framework rules as enactments that can inform the Matrix.

The Matrix hosts, like group psychoanalysts, cultivate negative capability (Bion, 1970), the ability to be in uncertainty without imposing ready-made answers. The hosts listen with benevolent neutrality, without judging, advising or guiding the group to any particular conclusion. They renounce the position of the expert—the subject who is supposed to know. Instead, they focus on dream telling and associations. By adopting this attitude, hosts encourage the same attitude in dreamers.

In addition, and similar to group psychoanalysts, hosts listen to the associative chain and phantasmatic resonance. The Matrix is similar to a 'stream of consciousness' (Manley, 2014, p. 331), in which dreams and associations resonate with each other, creating a multidimensional picture. Matrices also resonate with each other. The hosts listen to these resonances to discover hidden thoughts, meanings and relationships between dreams and reality (Manley, 2014). Consequently, they focus on the psychic reality of the Matrix as a whole to the detriment of its members and their links. Furthermore, because the *social dreaming matrix* is a non-psychoanalytic device, hosts offer working hypotheses about shared political and cultural realities. These hypotheses are not psychoanalytic interpretations of group transferences and anxieties unveiling repressed libidinal and aggressive drives, unfolding in the here and now of the Matrix experience, thereby generating insights into the foundation and dynamic Matrices as well as shared sociopolitical realities. These group interpretations, unlike individual cures, are ahistorical, focusing on current unconscious desires, defences and anxieties without returning to their infantile origins (Ezriel, as cited in Anzieu, 1984).

Hosts do not address group dynamics and transferences unless they become noisy and distract participants from the primary task of the Matrix. Furthermore, the hosts do not attend to their meta-position as observers or analyse their counter-transference and inter-transference (Kaës, 2004, 2015). Studying these group manifestations reduces resistance and interpreting them generates insight. Unaddressed group dynamics can jeopardise the primary task of the Matrix.

The dream reflection dialogue

At the end of a *social dreaming matrix*, the *dream reflection dialogue* is opened. In this moment, participants process the experience of the Matrix, exploring and identifying emerging emotions, thoughts and themes; they find links and advance working hypotheses related to the shared sociopolitical, organisational and human contexts, transforming unconscious thoughts into new knowledge (Manley, 2014). From a group psychoanalytic perspective, the *dream reflection dialogue* is a group session that primarily reflects on the *social dreaming matrix*. As such, it has specific group dynamics that resonate with those of the *social dreaming matrix*. Listening to the group dynamics that unfold in these sessions helps access the social unconscious and generate insight.

In a group psychoanalytic framework, similar to the role-playing moment of group psychodrama, the dynamics of the Matrix would not be interpreted so as not to disturb its dream-like state. During the *dream reflection dialogue*, the dynamics that unfolded in the Matrix and continued to unfold in the dialogue would be interpreted as an expression of the Matrix experience as a whole, its members and their links, to provide further knowledge about the different matrices within the *social unconscious*. The *dream reflection dialogue* would not be a forum for discussion that merely highlights emerging themes and generates working hypotheses. As such, this moment must be long enough to inform the Matrix.

Final remarks

The proposed group psychoanalytic approach to the *social dreaming matrix* envisages a framework that rediscovers and recreates the object *social dreaming matrix* proposed by Lawrence. This found-and-created device offers a psychoanalytic binocular vision approach to better envisage *social dreaming matrices* and *dream reflection dialogues*. It offers a broader perspective of the social unconscious that can generate further insights. As such, peacemakers and peacebuilders can use this complementary tool to protect and develop their practice.

References

Anzieu, D. (1984). *The group and the unconscious*. London: Routledge & Kegan Paul.
Baglioni, L., & Fubini, F. (2013). Social dreaming matrix. In: S. Long (Ed.), *Socioanalytic methods: Discovering the hidden in organisations and social systems* (pp. 107–129). London: Karnac Books.

Baranger, M., & Baranger, W. (2008). The analytic situation as a dynamic field. *The International Journal of Psychoanalysis, 89*(4): 795–826. https://doi.org/10.1111/j.1745-8315.2008.00074.x

Bion, W. R. (1961). *Experiences in groups and other papers.* London: Tavistock. https://doi.org/10.4324/9780203359075

Bion, W. R. (1963). *Elements of psychoanalysis.* London & New York: Routledge.

Bion, W. R. (1970). *Attention and interpretation: A scientific approach to insight in psychoanalysis and groups.* London: Tavistock.

Bion, W. R. (1984). *Elements of psychoanalysis.* London: Karnac.

Friedman, R. (2019). *Dream-telling, relations, and large groups: New developments in group analysis.* The new international library of group analysis (Kindle edition). London & New York: Routledge.

Hopper, E., & Weinberg, H. (2018). *The social unconscious in persons, groups and societies: Mainly theory.* The new international library of group analysis book (Kindle edition, Vol. 1). London & New York: Routledge.

Kaës, R. (2000). *L'appareil Psychique Groupal [The group psychic apparatus].* Paris: Dunod.

Kaës, R. (2002). *La Polyphonie du Rêve: L'expérience Onirique Commune et Partagée [The polyphony of dreams: The common and shared oneric experience].* Paris: Dunod.

Kaës, R. (2004). Intertransfert et analyse inter-transférentielle dans le travail psychanalytique conduit par plusieurs psychanalystes [Inter-transference and inter-transferential analysis in the psychoanalytic work led by several psychoanalysts]. *Filigrane, 13*(2): 5–15.

Kaës, R. (2015). *L'extension de la Psychanalyse: Pour une Métapsychologie de Troisième Type [The extension of psychoanalysis: For a metapsychology of the third type].* Paris: Dunod. https://doi.org/10.3917/dunod.kaes.2015.02

Kaës, R., Missenard, A., Nicolle, O., Benchimol, M., Blanchard, A.-M., Claquin, M., & Villier, J. (2003). *Le Psychodrame Psychanalytique de Groupe [Group psychoanalytic psychodrama].* Paris: Dunod.

Lawrence, W. G. (1998). *'Social Dreaming Matrix'@ Work.* London: Karnac.

Manley, J. (2010). Social dreaming in the 21st century: The world we are losing. *Organisational and Social Dynamics, 10*(1): 144–150.

Manley, J. (2014). Gordon Lawrence's 'Social Dreaming Matrix': Background, origins, history, and developments. *Organisational & Social Dynamics, 14*(2): 322–341.

Noack, A. (2010). 'Social Dreaming Matrix': Competition or complementation to individual dreaming? *Journal of Analytical Psychology, 55*(5): 672–690.

Winnicott, D. W. (1953). Transitional objects and transitional phenomena—A study of the first not-me possession. *The International Journal of Psychoanalysis, 34*: 89–97.

Winnicott, D. W. (1965). The maturational processes and the facilitating environment: Studies in the theory of emotional development. *The International Psychoanalytical Library, 64*:1–276. London: The Hogarth Press and the Institute of Psychoanalysis.

Index

For Product Safety Concerns and Information please contact our EU
representative GPSR@taylorandfrancis.com
Taylor & Francis Verlag GmbH, Kaufingerstraße 24, 80331 München, Germany